PRESENTED TO:

....

FROM:

....

DATE:

10

MINUTES

IN THE WORD

Proverbs

ZONDERVAN

10 Minutes in the Word: Proverbs

Copyright © 2018 Zondervan

This title is also available as a Zondervan ebook.

Requests for information should be addressed to:

Zondervan, 3900 Sparks Dr. SE, Grand Rapids, Michigan 49546

Library of Congress Cataloging-in-Publication Data
ISBN 978-0-310-09194-3

Art direction: Kathy Mitchell
Interior design: Kristy Edwards

Printed in China

18 19 20 21 22   TIMS   10 9 8 7 6 5 4 3 2 1

Contents

Introduction

The book of Proverbs belongs to a category of Scripture that theologians refer to as the "wisdom literature" of the Old Testament. The purpose of the book is to help readers acquire and apply God's wisdom to daily living. In Proverbs, the words *wise* and *wisdom* appear at least 125 times.[1] Solomon is the primary author of the book, but there are also contributions by Agur and King Lemuel. It should come as no surprise that Solomon is the main writer since God granted his request for wisdom and he became the wisest man in Israel (1 Kings 3). It is the short and pithy sayings written by Solomon found in chapters 10–31 that most of us identify with when we think of "proverbs."[2]

The truths found in Proverbs address several areas of life, including enjoying healthy relationships, handling money, avoiding trouble, dealing with temptation, managing our feelings, exercising self-control over our speech, maintaining a happy home, and building godly character.[3] While all of us want to succeed in these areas, and none of us want to be foolish, because of our sin nature we struggle in making good decisions. The book of Proverbs teaches us how to become wise in daily living as we experience a relationship with Jesus Christ. Only when our relationship with God is restored through Christ can we live wisely.

The Beginning of Knowledge

The fear of the LORD is the beginning of knowledge,
but fools despise wisdom and instruction.

—*Proverbs 1:7*

Read Proverbs 1:1–7

T he book of Proverbs doesn't waste any time stating its purpose. The opening verses reveal the goal is for gaining wisdom and instruction. The Hebrew word for "wisdom" is *hokmah* and is defined as "skill or expertise in living."[4] On any given day, there are countless opportunities to make either wise or foolish decisions. Wisdom is the ability to survey a situation and make the right choice. According to Solomon, a wise person makes a habit of listening and learning. When it comes to wisdom, there are always new things to learn. A wise person understands wisdom is not a destination where someone "arrives" but is a lifelong pursuit.

Possessing biblical wisdom isn't limited to people with high IQs and lofty degrees. Solomon revealed it's for those who are simple and young and are therefore naïve and untaught (v. 4), as well as those who are wise and discerning (v. 5). All people have the opportunity to grow in wisdom, instruction, and understanding.

While it's true most of us want to excel in every area of life, due to our sin nature, we lack the ability to make wise decisions. When a person attempts to be wise by drawing on his own resources, the best wisdom he can produce is "earthly, unspiritual, demonic" (James 3:15). Fools despise wisdom and instruction. Foolishness is doing what is right in your own eyes. Wisdom is doing things God's way.

You might be wondering, *How do I get wisdom?* Solomon instructed, "The fear of the LORD is the beginning of wisdom" (Proverbs 9:10). The phrase "fear of the LORD" is found fourteen times in Proverbs. In this context, the "fear of the LORD" doesn't mean being afraid of God. It means to esteem God above all things. Revering God above everything else is the first step in acquiring wisdom. This means there is no division between the sacred and secular parts of life, but rather, God governs every aspect of living. Practically speaking, when someone "fears the Lord" it means his relationship with God impacts every decision, and there is a desire to do things God's way. Wise living means relying on God rather than yourself (Proverbs 3:5–6).

Lord, help me understand that wisdom is a result of my relationship with You. Give me a heart and mind that revere You above all things. Empower me to prioritize my life in such a way that nothing comes before You. I ask You to increase my wisdom (James 1:5). Father, I also ask that You will give me a spirit of wisdom and revelation in the knowledge of You (Ephesians 1:17–18) and that I will increase in wisdom all the days of my life.

Do you long for the instruction of the Lord? Do you think you are always right, or are you open to correction? Is wisdom something you are willing to request from God? Acquiring wisdom is a worthy pursuit, but it takes time. The proverbs teach that wisdom cannot be attained apart from reverence for God. It is in Jesus Christ, "in whom are hidden all the treasures of wisdom and knowledge" (Colossians 2:3).

Listening Is a Skill

Listen, my son, to your father's instruction
    and do not forsake your mother's teaching.
They are a garland to grace your head
    and a chain to adorn your neck.

—*Proverbs 1:8-9*

It's no mistake that as Solomon introduced the topic of wisdom to his audience, one of the first commands he issued was to "listen." We've all known someone who was convinced he knew best and spurned the counsel of the wise. But no one will grow in wisdom without developing the skill of listening. Proverbs repeatedly issues the call to listen (4:1, 10, 20; 5:1, 7; 7:24; 8:32; 19:20; 22:17; 23:19, 22).

The first people we usually learn to take instruction from are our parents. But no amount of parental wisdom will help a child if he or she refuses to listen. Later in life, we have the opportunity to learn from teachers, coaches, pastors, bosses, and mentors. But our listening skills or lack of them will follow us to each relationship. The sooner we develop the ability to be a good listener, the better.

Solomon asserted that those who listen to instruction and apply wise teaching will be blessed. He wrote, "They are a garland to grace your head and a chain to adorn your neck" (v. 9). In Solomon's era, the garland and chain served as symbols of honor, guidance, and protection.[5] While it's true that none of us are promised a life free from struggles, those who choose to live wisely will avoid an enormous amount of trouble that routinely plagues those who live foolishly.

As we grow in wisdom and learn to listen well, we will be able to discern between wise counsel and bad advice. Not all the counsel we receive is biblically sound or even a good idea. Good listeners learn things that others don't. A former talk-show host once said, "I never learned anything while I was talking." Each day we have an opportunity to learn from other people. In fact, we can even learn from foolish people. As we watch and listen to foolish people speak, we can learn what to avoid. And, of course, as we watch and listen to the wise we can learn how to live well. A key component in becoming a good listener is admitting we still have things to learn. If we arrive at the false conclusion that we already know it all, we will talk more than we listen and never grow in wisdom.

Father, I acknowledge I have much to learn. I pray You will help me develop my listening skills and that I will be someone who is eager to learn. Teach me to be an active listener and give me a keen curiosity to learn new things.

How would you describe your listening skills? When someone speaks to you, are you engaged in what he or she is saying or are you focused on how you will respond? Do you approach each day with the possibility of learning something new? How would those closest to you describe your listening skills?

Wisdom Calls Out

Out in the open wisdom calls aloud,
    she raises her voice in the public square;
on top of the wall she cries out,
    at the city gate she makes her speech:
"How long will you who are simple love your simple
        ways?
    How long will mockers delight in mockery?"
—*Proverbs 1:20–22*

Read Proverbs 1:20–33

If you've ever set foot in Times Square in New York City or seen pictures of it in the media, you know it's an epicenter of advertising. Each billboard is larger than the next and competes to get the attention of the millions of people who pass through the tourist district each year. Solomon used similar imagery in regard to the call of wisdom. He wrote, "Out in the open wisdom calls aloud, she raises her voice in the public square; on top of the wall she cries out, at the city gate she makes her speech" (vv. 20–21).

In Solomon's era, the public square included a busy marketplace, and the city gate was the place where civic debate and official business took place. It was the location where knowledgeable people conducted commercial and legal business.[6] This imagery communicates that wisdom calls out to the masses. Wisdom is accessible to all people and not limited to the quiet studies of geniuses and scholars.

In the text, two questions are raised. First, "How long will you who are simple love your simple ways?" (v. 22a). Simple people are naïve and gullible, but not opposed to wisdom. The question is intended to encourage those who lack wisdom that there is a better way to live. The second question is, "How long will mockers delight in mockery and fools hate knowledge?" (v. 22b). Mockers are rebellious and reject the concept of wisdom and scorn those who are wise.

Both the simple and the mockers will find themselves on the wrong path. Wisdom issues an invitation, "Repent at my rebuke! Then I will pour out my thoughts to you, I will make known to you my teachings" (v. 23). Wisdom calls out, and we have a choice whether to accept the invitation or to continue in foolishness. Those who decline the invitation will be overcome with calamity (v. 27), but those who receive the invitation will live without fear of harm (v. 33).

Father, thank You that wisdom issues an invitation to all people and isn't kept from the simple or the foolish. Teach me to pursue Your wisdom and to turn from my foolish ways. I pray You will increase my desire for Your wisdom and that I would seek You all the days of my life.

What is your response to wisdom's invitation? Practically speaking, what are ways you can pursue wisdom? Do you spend time in God's Word? Are you in a small-group Bible study where you have the opportunity to grow alongside other believers? Do you regularly ask God to increase your wisdom?

Wisdom Is from the Lord

For the LORD gives wisdom;
    from his mouth come knowledge and
        understanding.
—*Proverbs 2:6*

Read Proverbs 2

American culture is obsessed with doing things quickly. We demand high-speed Internet, instant access, fast food, and overnight shipping. If a company doesn't meet our demand for speed, we take our business elsewhere. When we are forced to wait, many of us suspect something has gone wrong. Spiritually speaking, this mind-set is a liability. Proverbs 2 communicates that wisdom must be sought after over an extended period. It's a pursuit that requires time and patience. God is faithful to increase wisdom for those who pursue it, but we won't become wise overnight.

In the opening remarks of Proverbs 2, the word *if* appears three times in four verses. Solomon stated clearly that wisdom is ours for the seeking, but conditions must be met to obtain it. He wrote, "If you accept my words and store up my commands within you" (v. 1); "If you call out for insight and cry aloud for understanding" (v. 3); "If you look for it as for silver and search for it as for hidden treasure" (v. 4). Solomon was communicating to his readers that wisdom must be pursued. Obtaining wisdom demands time and effort. Wisdom won't just fall in our laps, and we can't expect it to arrive as quickly as we'd prefer. It may seem like a paradox, but wisdom is both a gift from God (v. 6) and a virtue that must be sought (vv. 1–5).

Solomon didn't just tell his readers how to pursue wisdom. He took it one step further and shared why we should pursue it. Solomon likely understood that most people don't like to be told what to do without an explanation as to why it's a good idea. Solomon shared several benefits of wisdom. Wisdom provides the ability to know what is just and right and the ability to instinctively know what path to take (v. 9). Wisdom and knowledge are pleasant to the soul (v. 10). Those who obtain a degree of wisdom will acquire a taste for it and long for more. The wise possess discretion that protects them from evil people (vv. 10–15). Wisdom can prevent those who possess it from falling into a trap and can save its recipients from adulterous relationships that destroy lives (vv. 10–18).

Father, I acknowledge You are the source of all wisdom and from Your mouth comes knowledge and understanding. Increase my desire to live wisely. As I read the Scriptures, open my eyes on how to apply Your ways to my everyday life. Allow me to acquire a taste for wisdom that motivates my pursuit.

God is the source of all wisdom, and He generously gives it to those who seek it. Spending time in God's Word is one of the primary ways to grow in wisdom. As you read the Scriptures, ask God to increase your wisdom as you study. Search for ways to apply the truths from God's Word to your everyday life. When you encounter situations, ask yourself, "What does God's Word say about this?"

Don't Follow Your Heart

Trust in the Lord with all your heart
　　and lean not on your own understanding;
in all your ways submit to him,
　　and he will make your paths straight.

—*Proverbs 3:5-6*

Read Proverbs 3:1–12

There's a good chance you've heard it said, "Follow your heart." It's a popular saying that promotes the idea that your heart will lead you in the right direction. The people who support this notion are probably well-intended, but it's terrible advice and has the potential to produce a disastrous outcome. The Bible teaches the human heart can't be trusted. The prophet Jeremiah wrote, "The heart is deceitful above all things and beyond cure. Who can understand it?" (Jeremiah 17:9). Our hearts are prone to lead us in a direction that feels right at the moment but ignore long-term consequences. As Christians, we aren't called to follow our hearts. We are called to follow Jesus.

Solomon instructed his readers to trust God and depend on His guidance, rather than our tainted inclinations (vv. 5–6). He cut to the chase in verse 7, "Do not be wise in your own eyes; fear the Lord and shun evil." The root of foolishness is thinking we are wiser than God. This fallacy can be traced all the way back to the garden of Eden (Genesis 3).[7] God's wisdom differs from the wisdom of humans. For instance, the Word of God commands us to humble ourselves before God (1 Peter 5:6), but human wisdom dictates that to be successful we must make a name for ourselves. Human wisdom insists that if you aren't first, you are last, but the

Word of God says, "So the last will be first, and the first will be last" (Matthew 20:16). God's ways differ from our own.

Understanding our limitations is vital. It will be a struggle until we arrive at the realization that God knows far better how to manage our lives than we do. As we submit every area of our lives to God, we will grow in wisdom. Notice how Solomon said, "In all your ways submit to him, and he will make your paths straight" (v. 6). There's a temptation to seek God's wisdom in some areas of life and disregard it in others. But God calls us to submit every area of our life to His lordship. Partial obedience isn't obedience at all. Submission might sound oppressive, but in reality, it's just the opposite. Everything that God asks of us, He does because He wants to bless us or keep us from harm.[8]

Father, help me see that Your wisdom is far greater than any advice the world has to offer. Increase my trust in Your goodness. Help me submit every area of my life to Your authority and lead me to walk in Your ways.

Do you trust God or your own best guesses? Are there areas that you need to submit to Him? Have you concluded that God knows how to manage your life better than you do? If you are struggling in any of these areas, it's wise to ask God to open your eyes to your limitations. We won't fully embrace God's wisdom until we are convinced it's far superior to our limited understanding.

Wisdom Is Profitable

Blessed are those who find wisdom,
    those who gain understanding,
for she is more profitable than silver
    and yields better returns than gold.
She is more precious than rubies;
    nothing you desire can compare with her.
—*Proverbs 3:13–15*

I nsurance companies are profitable because people understand the necessity of insuring their most valuable assets. Most people carry insurance policies on their homes and cars so that in the event they are damaged or destroyed, they can be replaced. Art collectors who own rare and valuable paintings insure these pieces for exorbitant sums because they know they are irreplaceable. But how often do we contemplate the value of wisdom?

Solomon wrote that those who find wisdom are *blessed* (v. 13). In this instance, the word *blessed* is plural and might be rendered, "Oh the blessedness of those who find wisdom."[9] Solomon went on to say that wisdom and understanding are more profitable than silver and gold and more precious than rubies (vv. 14–15). Although silver and gold are undeniable measures of wealth, they only have the potential to obtain things that money can buy. Wisdom can acquire things money can't buy.

In the Old Testament, it was common for some Israelites to believe that wealth was a sign of God's blessing while poverty suggested a lack of God's favor. Of course, this wasn't the case because the Scriptures make it clear that God loves the poor. Solomon was communicating to his audience that there is a way to be enriched that has nothing to do with material possessions. Wisdom doesn't guarantee financial prosperity but instead brings imperishable blessings such as knowledge, discretion, prudence, humility, reverence, godly speech, and guidance.[10] These are significant assets that have extreme value but can't be purchased with money. There's nothing wrong with enjoying things that money can buy, as long as we place the higher value on the things money can't buy. Jesus said, "But seek first his kingdom and his righteousness, and all these things will be given to you as well" (Matthew 6:33).

Some people work hard their entire lives for material possessions that will perish. The book of Proverbs teaches us that the most valuable things in life can't be purchased with money. We have the option to choose what type of riches we pursue. Undoubtedly, wisdom doesn't come easily and must be sought, but we have the opportunity to seek wisdom with the same intensity as some who seek material wealth.

Father, I thank You that wisdom has incalculable value and that You give it to those who ask for it and seek it. I pray I will value wisdom more than silver or gold. Help me to remember that most things in this world will perish, but my relationship with You will last forever.

What value do you place on wisdom? What are your most treasured possessions? Are your most valued assets material or spiritual in nature? To what degree are you striving to obtain wisdom?

Wisdom Provides Peace of Mind

Have no fear of sudden disaster
    or of the ruin that overtakes the wicked,
for the Lord will be at your side
    and will keep your foot from being snared.
—*Proverbs 3:25–26*

Read Proverbs 3:25–35

In a culture that entertains a twenty-four-hour news cycle, many people live with a constant low-grade anxiety that something terrible is about to happen. Instant access to world events gives us plenty of reason to be concerned. Mass shootings, health epidemics, terrorism, hate crimes, conflicts between international governments, and troubles in the economy are frequent topics of conversation in our society. But the Bible repeatedly tells us not to fear. In this passage, Solomon was pointing to the benefits of wisdom and how it keeps us safe from sudden trouble.

Solomon instructed his son, "My son, do not let wisdom and understanding out of your sight, preserve sound judgment and discretion; they will be life for you, an ornament to grace your neck" (vv. 21–22). Wisdom leads us in a direction that is away from the wicked. It enables us to use sound judgment and avoid traps that unwise people often fall in. Solomon pointed out that when we make wise decisions, there is no need to fear the sudden disasters that overtake the wicked (v. 25). When we walk wisely, we will never stay awake at night wondering if we'll get caught. We'll never have to wonder, *How can I cover this up?* or, *What if I get found out?* Walking in wisdom keeps our consciences clear and our minds free from worry.[11]

Those who walk wisely can rest in the fact that the Lord will keep us from falling into traps set by the wicked (v. 26). We must always remember that a person isn't spared from disaster because of his or her competence or common sense. Rather, God's protection is the basis for our confidence. Although the wicked quickly come to ruin (v. 25), God's people are kept safe. We must be mindful that wise living doesn't mean nothing bad will ever happen to us. In fact, Jesus told His followers, "I have told you these things, so that in me you may have peace. In this world you will have trouble. But take heart! I have overcome the world" (John 16:33). But when we use sound judgment we eliminate many of the troubles that foolish people bring on themselves by making poor choices.

Father, I thank You that Your Word repeatedly tells us not to fear. Help me to make wise choices that keep me from foolish consequences. I pray You will increase my trust and that I will ultimately rely on You to keep me safe in every circumstance.

Is your life characterized more by faith or by fear? Practically speaking, what wise choices can you make in your life to avoid disasters? Do you correlate wisdom with safety and confidence?

Guard Your Heart

Above all else, guard your heart,
for everything you do flows from it.

—*Proverbs 4:23*

....

E ach year millions of people make appointments with cardiologists to have their hearts examined. Symptoms such as heart palpitations, shortness of breath, and tightness in the chest are all indications something is wrong. Oftentimes medication, surgery, or changes in lifestyle can fix the problem. In the book of Proverbs, the heart is regarded as the center of an individual's inner life. The heart is where thoughts, feelings, and choices originate.[12] From a spiritual perspective, the condition of our hearts manifests itself in our behavior.

Jesus said, "A good man brings good things out of the good stored up in his heart, and an evil man brings evil things out of the evil stored up in his heart. For the mouth speaks what the heart is full of" (Luke 6:45). Since our heart is the epicenter of our inner life and it dictates our behavior, it's understandable that Solomon warned his readers to guard their hearts above all things.

Spiritually speaking, we are all born with a heart problem. Since the fall of man (Genesis 3) we have all rebelled and fallen short of the glory of God (Romans 3:23). Christ's salvation is the only remedy for our heart problem. Only Jesus can fix what is broken. After we become Christians, we must continue to guard our hearts. The Scriptures instruct us to avoid a deceptive heart (Psalm 12:2), a hard heart (Proverbs 28:14), an unbelieving heart (Hebrews 3:12), a cold heart (Matthew 24:12), and an impure heart (Psalm 51:10).[13]

It's with good reason that Solomon warned us to guard our hearts. Everything we see, hear, and think about makes its way to our hearts. We are the gatekeepers to our hearts, and what we allow in is our choice. If we choose to consume a steady diet of ungodly substance, we shouldn't be surprised when it rears its ugly head in our behavior. On the other hand, if we steadily ingest the Scriptures, biblical preaching, and resources that increase our wisdom, we can expect for our hearts and behavior to respond accordingly.

Father, I pray You will help me to guard my heart. As the psalmist prayed, "Create in me a pure heart, O God, and renew a steadfast spirit within me" (Psalm 51:10). Help me to make godly choices in what I watch for entertainment, and I pray You will be quick to convict and redirect me when I cross the line.

As we grow in wisdom, we will become increasingly mindful of what we allow to permeate our hearts. Wise living demands intentionality. Are you mindful that the things we intellectually consume have a dramatic impact on the heart? Do you use discretion? What steps do you need to take to guard your heart? Guarding our hearts isn't just about avoiding things. It's also about providing our hearts with truth from God's Word that results in wisdom.

A Path That Leads to Destruction

For the lips of the adulterous woman drip honey,
and her speech is smoother than oil;
but in the end she is bitter as gall,
sharp as a double-edged sword.
Her feet go down to death;
her steps lead straight to the grave.
—*Proverbs 5:3–5*

Read Proverbs 5

Our society holds a lax view about sex. The prevailing attitude is that anything goes. As long as no one gets hurt, anything is acceptable. But of course, people do get hurt. Countless people suffer from broken hearts, shame and regret, unplanned pregnancies, sexually transmitted diseases, and marital infidelity. God takes sexual sin seriously. He knows that sex outside the bonds of marriage is detrimental to the human soul. God intends for sex to be enjoyed only in the context of marriage. He communicated the importance of marital faithfulness by addressing the topic in the Ten Commandments. The seventh commandment says, "You shall not commit adultery" (Exodus 20:14).

King Solomon was a man who sinned in this area more than most. First Kings 11:3 says, "He had seven hundred wives of royal birth and three hundred concubines, and his wives led him astray." Solomon learned the hard way that adultery leads to disaster. In Proverbs 5 he was writing to his son and pleading with him to avoid sexual activity outside the bonds of covenant marriage. Undoubtedly, Solomon wanted his son to avoid the trap he had fallen in.

Solomon warned that sexual unfaithfulness begins with flattering communication. Both men and women thrive on attention and admiration. Human beings are prone to fall for flattery.[14] It might begin in a subtle way that seems harmless. Perhaps a coworker offers compliments or a sympathetic ear. Or maybe someone you used to date reaches out on social media and lavishes you with attention. In the beginning, the communication seems harmless and fun. Solomon described an adulterous woman's lips as ones that "drip honey" and her speech is "smoother than oil" (v. 3). But those words serve as a bait and switch. What begins in fun ends in sorrow. Solomon wrote that in the end her words are "bitter as gall" (v. 4) (gall was the most bitter substance in Jewish culture) and "her feet go down to death" (v. 5). Adultery may lead to a literal death, or Solomon's words may be referring to a metaphorical death of a life of peace and harmony.[15]

Father, I pray You will guard my heart and mind against sexual immorality. I pray I will only have a love and attraction for my spouse. Should I find myself tempted, I pray You will give me the wisdom to flee immediately. I pray that I will honor my marriage and my marriage bed will be kept pure, for You will judge the adulterer and the sexually immoral (Hebrews 13:4).

Sexual temptation should be taken seriously. In fact, God warns His people to run from sexual temptation. Paul wrote, "Flee from sexual immorality. All other sins a person commits are outside the body, but whoever sins sexually, sins against their own body" (1 Corinthians 6:18). Solomon offered similar instruction in Proverbs 5:8: "Keep to a path far from her, do not go near the door of her house." Adultery leads to disgrace and ruin. Those who are wise look ahead to where a path will lead.

Just a Little Might Be Too Much

How long will you lie there, you sluggard?
   When will you get up from your sleep?
A little sleep, a little slumber,
   a little folding of the hands to rest—
and poverty will come on you like a thief
   and scarcity like an armed man.
—*Proverbs 6:9-11*

T he road to wise living is narrow, but there are a variety of paths that lead to destruction. Proverbs 6 warns of three threats that can destroy our lives: foolish financial decisions (vv. 1–5), laziness (vv. 6–11), and lust (vv. 20–35). The poet Robert Frost didn't avoid the topic of laziness. Frost said, "The world is full of willing people: some willing to work, the rest willing to let them."[16] The Bible makes it clear that God's people are called to have an excellent work ethic. The apostle Paul went as far as to say that if a person isn't willing to work, he or she shouldn't eat (2 Thessalonians 3:10).

In the Bible, a sluggard is the opposite of a diligent person. He or she is a slacker who avoids work or does as little as possible. Unlike the oppressed who suffer poverty because of circumstances beyond their control, the sluggard's poverty is a result of his choices. The sluggard chooses sleep over work (vv. 9–10). He might rationalize sleeping in and frequent naps as "just a little," but they destroy his productivity. As a result of his idleness, poverty comes on him like a "thief" or an "armed man" (v. 11). In other words, poverty arrives in a manner that is sudden and unexpected.

Solomon instructed the lazy person to consider the ways of an ant (v. 6). An ant makes progress little by little as it diligently makes provision for the future. The ant requires no supervision and does the work without being prompted (vv. 7–8). Some people go to work each day and do the bare minimum. When the boss is out of the office, they do even less. Diligent people plan their day and then work hard to finish. Proverbs 21:5 says, "The plans of the diligent lead to profit as surely as haste leads to poverty."

The first thing God revealed about Himself in the Scriptures is that He is a God who is at work (Genesis 1). As image bearers of God, human beings are designed to do excellent work. Christians not only are to avoid laziness but should also be the most productive employees in the workplace. Whether or not we like our boss or the work we are doing is not a factor. We are still commanded to do our best. Paul wrote, "Whatever you do, work at it with all your heart, as working for the Lord, not for human masters, since you know that you will receive an inheritance from the Lord as a reward. It is the Lord Christ you are serving" (Colossians 3:23–24).

Father, I thank You for the work You have given me to do. I pray You will help me approach my work with diligence. Help me to remember my work is an offering to You. I ask that You will convict me of areas in my life where I am lazy or not doing my best work. Empower me to have an excellent work ethic.

Do you work diligently or do just the bare minimum? How might your work life change if you approached each day with the attitude that you were performing your work for God?

Beware of Adultery

But a man who commits adultery has no sense;
   whoever does so destroys himself.
Blows and disgrace are his lot,
   and his shame will never be wiped away.
For jealousy arouses a husband's fury,
   and he will show no mercy when he takes
      revenge.
—Proverbs 6:32–34

When God commands His people to avoid something, it's not because He wants to keep us from enjoyment; it's because it has the potential to destroy us. Time and again the book of Proverbs warns its readers about the perils of adultery. Immorality always leads to pain, and no one escapes its consequences.

Some people believe that if they don't get caught cheating, they will avoid the consequences of adultery, but that isn't true. Solomon asked his readers two rhetorical questions, "Can a man scoop fire into his lap without his clothes being burned? Can a man walk on hot coals without his feet being scorched? So is he who sleeps with another man's wife, no one who touches her will go unpunished" (vv. 27–29). Solomon's point is, pain is inevitable. It's impossible to commit adultery and remain unscathed or go unpunished.

Solomon described a person who commits adultery as one who has no sense (v. 32a). Not only does infidelity devastate spouses', children's, and family members' lives, but it also destroys the one who engages in immorality (v. 32b). Engaging in adultery demonstrates a self-destructive urge that shows a lack of judgment. An extramarital affair may provide initial excitement and short-term satisfaction, but the long-term consequences will be incalculable.[17]

One poor decision can destroy trust that took a lifetime to build. Sometimes the damage is beyond repair.

There are some acts of immorality that, because of extenuating circumstances, can be understood by outsiders. For instance, if a person steals because he or his family is starving, he will have to pay the penalty for his crime, but it's not likely he will lose the respect of the community (v. 30). This isn't the case with adultery. Extramarital affairs destroy reputations. Solomon wrote of the adulterer, "Blows and disgrace are his lot, and his shame will never be wiped away" (v. 33). A court of law can be satisfied if an offender does his time and pays his fines, but a jealous husband's wrath will never be satisfied (v. 34). God warns His people to avoid adultery at all costs because it devastates people.

Father, I thank You for the gift of marriage. I pray You will guard my marriage from anything that has the potential to harm it. Give me the wisdom I need to avoid adultery. Teach me to flee at the first inclination of temptation.

Whether you are married or single, what steps can you take to guard yourself against adultery? Do you respect other people's marriages? Do you protect your marriage? What signals do you send that communicate you honor your marriage vows and the vows of others?

Dealing with Temptation

My son, keep my words
   and store up my commands within you.
Keep my commands and you will live;
   guard my teachings as the apple of your eye.
Bind them on your fingers;
   write them on the tablet of your heart.
—*Proverbs 7:1–3*

Everyone deals with temptation. In Proverbs 7, Solomon instructed his son on how to guard himself against an adulterous woman. Temptation comes in a variety of forms, but the counsel Solomon offered lends itself as an effective way of dealing with all types of temptation. Wise people assume temptation will be a lifelong issue and take drastic measures to guard against it. If we think we are immune to temptation, we are especially vulnerable.

Solomon instructed his readers to "store up my commands within you" (v. 1). One of the most effective weapons in dealing with temptation is Scripture memorization. When the Enemy tempted Jesus, the Lord retaliated by quoting from the book of Deuteronomy (Matthew 4). On three separate occasions, Jesus responded by saying, "It is written." Jesus resisted the devil by standing firmly on God's Word. If we want to overcome temptation, we must know what the Word of God says and be able to call it to memory in times of testing.

Most of us have a good idea of the areas in which we are prone to temptation. It's wise to identify specific passages in Scripture that address our areas of weakness and memorize those verses. It's imperative to decide in advance how to respond to temptation. Temptation often catches us off guard. If we've determined a response ahead of time, we have a far better chance of avoiding failure. As with all things, Christ is our example. Jesus was committed to doing His Father's will. Not only did He know Scripture and quote the Scriptures, but He obeyed the Word of God in times of testing. Solomon wrote, "Keep my commands and you will live; guard my teachings as the apple of your eye" (Proverbs 7:2). It's not enough just to know the Word of God. To avoid falling into the trap of temptation, we must also obey it.

Whenever possible, it's wise to avoid situations that are known to lead to temptation. When Solomon warned against the seduction of the adulterous woman, he wrote, "Do not let your heart turn to her ways or stray into her paths" (v. 25). If we can avoid tempting circumstances, we should make every attempt to do so. Intentionally placing ourselves in places we know we will be tempted is foolish. It will serve us well to think through the impending consequences if we succumb to temptations. Solomon warned of the adulteress, "Her house is a highway to the grave, leading down to the chambers of death" (v. 27). The simple act of thinking through where our choices lead us is beneficial. Relying on God's Word to strengthen us and using wisdom to avoid temptation will go a long way in dealing with temptation.

Father, I pray You will increase my wisdom in dealing with temptation. Let the Word of God dwell richly in my heart so I can be quick to recall it in times of need. I pray for the wisdom to avoid situations that I know will tempt me to sin.

In what areas are you prone to temptation? Are you mindful of the specific Bible passages that address temptation? What steps can you take to memorize applicable passages of Scripture?

Knowing What to Embrace and Avoid

"I, wisdom, dwell together with prudence;
    I possess knowledge and discretion.
To fear the Lᴏʀᴅ is to hate evil;
    I hate pride and arrogance,
        evil behavior and perverse speech."
—*Proverbs 8:12–13*

Read Proverbs 8:1–13

One of the advantages of wisdom is it teaches us what to embrace and what to avoid. Wisdom doesn't come solo. Along with wisdom come a variety of other virtues, such as prudence, knowledge, and discretion (v. 12). Prudence can be defined as good and sensible behavior, while knowledge characterizes not only academic ability but also knowledge of the truth. In the book of Proverbs, discretion can be described as careful behavior that comes from clear thinking. All three of these virtues refer to the ability to carry out sound plans.[18] The characteristics that accompany wisdom are attributes wise people embrace.

Wisdom also teaches us what to avoid. As we grow in our relationship with the Lord, we start to love the same things He loves and hate the same things He hates. Things that grieve the heart of God will grieve us. When this occurs, it's a sign of spiritual growth. The apostle Paul wrote, "The person with the Spirit makes judgments about all things, but such a person is not subject to merely human judgments, for, 'Who has known the mind of the Lord so as to instruct him?' But we have the mind of Christ" (1 Corinthians 2:15–16).

Those who have the mind of Christ begin to view evil the same way God does.

Solomon wrote, "To fear the LORD is to hate evil: I hate pride and arrogance, evil behavior and perverse speech" (Proverbs 8:13). As God's people, we are called to humble ourselves under His authority. Pride, arrogance, evil behavior, and perverse speech all show a lack of submission to God. Wise people attempt to avoid any behavior that God finds offensive. In Proverbs, one of the main purposes of the "fear of the LORD" is to align our hearts with what God loves. As we grow in wisdom and learn what is offensive to Him, we can examine our hearts and ask God to guard us against such things.

Although wisdom is for everyone, those who receive the benefits of wisdom are those who love and seek her. "I love those who love me, and those who seek me find me" (v. 17).

Father, I thank You that wisdom teaches us both what to embrace and what to avoid. I pray You will give me a heart that loves what You love and hates what You hate. I pray You will remove everything in my character that is offensive to You.

Do you find yourself grieved over things that grieve the heart of God? Do you love what He loves and hate what He hates? Can you name any specific things you try to avoid because those things are offensive to God?

Wisdom Is a Person

Listen to my instruction and be wise;
do not disregard it.
Blessed are those who listen to me,
watching daily at my doors,
waiting at my doorway.
For those who find me find life
and receive favor from the Lord.
But those who fail to find me harm themselves;
all who hate me love death.
—*Proverbs 8:33–36*

P roverbs 8 reveals to us that the book of Proverbs doesn't
simply represent Solomon's wisdom, but instead, it represents God's wisdom.[19] The New Testament teaches that Jesus is
the wisdom of God (1 Corinthians 1:24, 30). With this in mind,
Proverbs 8 encourages readers to be in a relationship with Christ.
It's impossible to become wise apart from Christ because He is the
source of all wisdom.

In Solomon's teaching, he used the personification of Woman
Wisdom. He presented her as female since the Hebrew word for
"wisdom" is a feminine noun, and the audience of Solomon's
teaching was a young man.[20] Wisdom isn't limited to only a personification of Solomon's wisdom. It includes the wisdom God
used to create the universe.

Solomon's personification of wisdom reveals that Woman
Wisdom places herself at the busiest entrance to the city and issues
a loud invitation to the crowd (vv. 1–4). She competes with the
immoral woman (Proverbs 5–7) and Woman Folly (Proverbs 9).
She stands at a crossroads, where people are forced to make a decision. The invitation is issued to all of humanity, even the most
simple and foolish (8:4–5), and she offers to teach them common

sense. Woman Wisdom understands the way the world works (vv. 6–9) and discerns the difference between good and evil.

Woman Wisdom has desirable companions that she shares, which include prudence, knowledge, and discretion (v. 12). These are the friends Woman Wisdom associates with, but she also instructs what to avoid. Woman Wisdom hates evil, pride, arrogance, evil behavior, and perverse speech (v. 13). Counsel and sound judgment originate with wisdom, along with insight and power (v. 14).

Not only is acquiring wisdom essential, but so is receiving the blessings that are attached to it. Riches and honor, enduring wealth, and prosperity accompany wisdom (v. 18). This shouldn't be confused with the heresy of the prosperity gospel, since these blessings may not come to us in this world, but in the next. Wisdom communicates that what she produces in us (wisdom and righteousness) is better than financial prosperity.[21]

Father, thank You that You have chosen to reveal the source of all wisdom in the person and finished work of Jesus Christ. Teach me to follow Jesus in such a way that I walk closely enough to learn His ways, develop His character, and reflect His wisdom.

Solomon used Proverbs 8 to personify wisdom in a way that the reader relates to a gracious woman. But the message of the gospel is that Jesus Christ, the source of all wisdom, took on flesh (John 1:14) and dwelt among us. The God who spoke the universe into existence wants to have a relationship with us. Only in Christ can we learn to live wisely, take the right paths, and grow in wisdom in righteousness. Jesus is the source of all wisdom. The way to walk in wisdom is to follow Jesus Christ.

Don't Waste Your Breath

Whoever corrects a mocker invites insults;
> whoever rebukes the wicked incurs abuse.

Do not rebuke mockers or they will hate you;
> rebuke the wise and they will love you.

Instruct the wise and they will be wiser still;
> teach the righteous and they will add to their
> learning.

—*Proverbs 9:7–9*

Read Proverbs 9:1–12

P roverbs 9 is the climax for the introduction of the book. Up until this point, Woman Wisdom and the immoral woman (also known as folly) have been competing for the son's affection.[22] For all of us, it boils down to this question: Will you choose the way of wisdom or folly? The decision has an enormous impact. Whether we choose to walk in the way of wisdom or the way of folly will influence every aspect of life. Our degree of wisdom or lack of it will even determine how we communicate with others.

The way of wisdom teaches to avoid correcting a mocker because the mocker resists sound judgment and will respond with verbal abuse. The mocker hates those who correct him or her (vv. 7–8). Wise people don't waste their breath correcting a mocker because it's a waste of time. Mockers don't listen. Correcting a mocker isn't effective, and it invites verbal barbs. Some people refuse wise counsel and will never submit to authority. On the other hand, a wise person embraces correction. Wise people are always looking for ways to improve, so they appreciate the feedback. In fact, the text says, "Rebuke the wise and they will love you" (v. 8).

According to verses 7–9, we need wisdom to discern when to correct and when to stay quiet. The way to proceed is by predicting the likely outcome. Most of us have a pretty good idea of how someone will respond when corrected. Is this a person who will respond defensively and with contempt? Or will he be glad to receive instruction because it will make him better? Wise people can size up a situation and determine whether or not offering counsel will help or make things worse.

On a personal level, these verses might be revealing. If you have trouble receiving correction, you are a mocker. If you get defensive when corrected, you are a mocker. If you respond to a rebuke by verbally abusing the person who did the rebuking, you are a mocker. However, if you are willing to hear someone out and then carefully contemplate if there is any truth in the correction, you are wise. If you appreciate counsel that might be difficult to hear but will make you better, you are wise. If you would prefer to be corrected than continue in ignorance, you are wise.

Father, I pray You will give me discernment to know when to speak up and when to remain quiet. Help me to have the wisdom to know the difference between a mocker and a wise person. Empower me to hold my tongue in the presence of a mocker. If I possess the traits of a mocker, I pray for correction and the humility to learn and grow.

Proverbs 9 makes it clear that if you can't accept correction, it has nothing to do with your personality type. It's a symptom of pride and idolatry of self. If that's true of you, the starting point on the road to wisdom is a relationship with Christ (v. 10). If you are immersed in folly, you don't have to remain there. "Does not wisdom call out? Does not understanding raise her voice?" (Proverbs 8:1).

Two Invitations: Wisdom or Folly

Folly is an unruly woman;
    she is simple and knows nothing.
She sits at the door of her house,
    on a seat at the highest point of the city,
calling out to those who pass by,
    who go straight on their way.

—Proverbs 9:13–15

A t some point, all of us have experienced the dilemma of receiving two invitations to different events that take place at the same time. Since it's impossible to be in both places simultaneously, we had to make a decision on which invitation to accept. In the same way, "Woman Wisdom" and "Woman Folly" issue two invitations that lead to very different places, and we, too, must decide which invitation we will accept and which one to decline.

In Proverbs 8, we saw that Woman Wisdom placed herself at the busiest entrance to the city and extended a loud invitation to the crowd (vv. 1–4). Similarly, Woman Folly in Proverbs 9 sits on a seat at the highest point in the city and calls out to those who are passing by and invites them to a feast (vv. 14–15, 17). Solomon described her as unruly, simple, and someone who knows nothing, but still, she persists (v. 13). Woman Folly mimics the invitation of Woman Wisdom to gain the attention of her targeted victims, but the menu she offers is radically different. Rather than meat and wine (v. 2), she serves water that is stolen and bread that must be eaten in secret (v. 17). Folly's invitation may initially sound exciting, but death is on the other side of her door (v. 18).

Proverbs 9 issues two party invitations: one hosted by Woman Wisdom and the other by Woman Folly. One of these parties leads to abundant life, and the other leads to death.[23] The New Testament teaches that Jesus is the wisdom of God (1 Corinthians 1:24, 30), and He invites us to a meal as well. John 6:35 says, "Then Jesus declared, 'I am the bread of life. Whoever comes to me will never go hungry, and whoever believes in me will never be thirsty.'" Christ's meal is not for those who already think they are wise, but for those who know they are in desperate need of Christ and His wisdom. Jesus lived a sinless and perfectly wise life, yet He took the punishment our foolishness deserved (Romans 5:8). When we believe in Christ's death and resurrection and follow Him as Lord, He increases our wisdom. It's an invitation we accept or decline. Jesus answered, "I am the way and the truth and the life. No one comes to the Father except through me" (John 14:6).

Father, thank You for extending an invitation to me to sit at Your table. I pray You will increase my wisdom and give me the insight to reject all invitations of folly. Help me to grow in my love for Christ and live in a way that is pleasing to You.

Do you believe that Christ is the source of all wisdom? Are you on the path of wisdom or the path of folly?

Wisdom with Money and Work

Ill-gotten treasures have no lasting value,
   but righteousness delivers from death.
The Lord does not let the righteous go hungry,
   but he thwarts the craving of the wicked.
Lazy hands make for poverty,
   but diligent hands bring wealth.
He who gathers crops in summer is a prudent son,
   but he who sleeps during harvest is a disgraceful
      son.
—*Proverbs 10:2–5*

Read Proverbs 10:1–12

The book of Proverbs has a lot to say about how to manage work and money. Foolish people are greedy and will do unethical things to acquire money. Some people cheat on their taxes, steal from their employers, and make shady business deals in the pursuit of wealth. But Solomon said in verse 2, "Ill-gotten treasures have no lasting value." In other words, what we manipulate to get is not ours to keep. From God's perspective, how we acquire our possessions is more important than what we possess.

We've all heard about high-profile swindlers who got away with embezzling millions of dollars. We might be tempted to believe they will go unpunished, but that's not true. The key to understanding the truths of Proverbs is to interpret them in view of Christ and eternity, rather than with immediate consequences.[24] In this world, evil people might make money while righteous people starve, but in the end, those who are in Christ will be without trouble, and those apart from Christ will suffer.

Along with how to rightly earn money comes the topic of work. Solomon blatantly warned against laziness. "Lazy hands make for poverty, but diligent hands bring wealth" (v. 4). Sadly, most people don't recognize their own laziness. A modern-day perception of laziness is someone who stays on the couch all day, watching TV.

In Proverbs, a lazy person is associated with someone who can't see a project through to the finish line.[25] In verse 5, Solomon used the example of a son who is present to gather crops in the summer but sleeps during the harvest. His poor work ethic brings disgrace to his parents.

In our society, distraction is a problem that prevents us from finishing tasks. Overcommitted schedules, social media, entertainment, and a lack of focus are all threats to our work life. Finishing any task requires persistence. The opposite of laziness is diligence. Diligent people keep working until a job is completed. A lazy person begins multiple projects but fails to finish.

None of us want to be foolish with money. We also don't want to have a reputation for being lazy. We need wisdom to handle money well and to enjoy an excellent work ethic. This type of wisdom typically comes from earning money a little at a time and working hard over a prolonged period (Proverbs 13:11).

Father, I want to earn and manage money in a way that brings You honor. I pray You will increase my wisdom in the area of my finances. I ask You to empower me to be diligent in my work and to work with excellence. Help me to see projects through to completion and to do my best work.

Are you wise when it comes to money management or do you lack self-control? Do you see tasks through to completion or do you abandon them before they are finished? How would you describe your work ethic? Wisdom is not only knowing the right thing to do but also having the ability to carry it out. How can you apply wisdom to your money and work?

The Value of Discernment

Wisdom is found on the lips of the discerning,
   but a rod is for the back of one who has no sense.
The wise store up knowledge,
   but the mouth of a fool invites ruin.
—*Proverbs 10:13–14*

Read Proverbs 10:13–32

Discernment is the ability to distinguish between truth and error. It's an inner knowing that allows us to decipher between wisdom and foolishness.[26] Imagine the heartache and trouble that might be avoided for those with good discernment. According to Solomon, those with discernment speak words of wisdom that are helpful to other people, but those who lack it say things that bring punishment (v. 13). Wisdom and discernment provide us the ability to see danger and avoid it. It also gives us insight into the situations we find ourselves in.

In the New Testament, the apostle Paul prayed for the believers at Philippi to grow in their knowledge and ability to discern what is best. He wrote, "This is my prayer: that your love may abound more and more in knowledge and depth of insight, so that you may be able to discern what is best and may be pure and blameless for the day of Christ" (Philippians 1:9–10).

As Christians, it's not uncommon for us to take our needs to God in prayer. We ask for favor at work, for good test results when we are sick, for mortgages to be approved, for our children to do well in school, and for a variety of other temporal comforts. Undoubtedly, we should ask God for these things. The Scriptures encourage us to "cast all [our] anxiety on him" (1 Peter 5:7). But what if we broadened our prayer requests? What if we asked for more than temporal comforts? What if, like Paul, we asked for spiritual growth that resulted in valuable things such as wisdom and discernment?

The Scriptures give us permission to expand our prayer lives and encourage us to pray for our spiritual vitality. If we were to do a study of the prayers Paul prayed at the beginning of the New Testament letters he wrote, we'd see he continually prayed for the spiritual growth of those he served. Paul wasn't the only one who prayed for spiritual vitality. James wrote, "If any of you lacks wisdom, you should ask God, who gives generously to all without finding fault, and it will be given to you" (James 1:5). Spiritual growth and vitality are gifts from God. We are wise to ask for them.

Father, I thank You for the gift of prayer. I thank You that I can come to You with all my needs and requests. Help me to expand my prayer life. I pray You will increase my wisdom, knowledge, and discernment. I ask You to make me as hungry for spiritual growth as I am for temporal comforts.

What are your most frequent prayer requests? How can you expand your prayer life to include areas of spiritual growth? How might your life be different if you consistently prayed for spiritual growth in your life and for those you love? Are you confident these are requests God will be pleased to answer?

The Sin of All Sins

When pride comes, then comes disgrace,

but with humility comes wisdom.

—*Proverbs 11:2*

P ride is at the root of all sin. Many biblical scholars believe that pride is the "sin of all sins" because it was pride that caused Lucifer to say, "I will make myself like the Most High" (Isaiah 14:14).[27] In Eden, the Enemy tempted Eve by appealing to her pride. He said, "You will be like God, knowing good and evil" (Genesis 3:5). Eve took the bait, and the result was the fall of man (Genesis 3). Ever since the fall, human beings have craved honor and recognition that are due to God alone. Biblical commentator William Barclay said, "Pride is the ground in which all other sins grow, and the parent from which all the other sins come."[28]

Pride has been described as "self-centeredness" turned outward.[29] Ultimately, pride always loses what it seeks. A prideful person seeks honor but brings disgrace on himself (11:2). In Proverbs 25 Solomon illustrated the human propensity for seeking praise and recognition by writing about honey: "If you find honey, eat just enough—too much of it, and you will vomit" (v. 16), and "It is not good to eat too much honey, nor is it honorable to search out matters that are too deep" (v. 27). If honey represents recognition and praise, Solomon warned too much will make us sick. Human beings are not capable of receiving excessive amounts of praise and honor without damage being done. Our egos and psyches weren't wired to handle fame. Perhaps that's why it's common for so many celebrities to find themselves in a world of heartache.

Solomon's most quoted words on the topic of pride are, "Pride goes before destruction, a haughty spirit before a fall" (Proverbs 16:18). Time and again the Scriptures warn about the dangers of pride. Pride puts us at odds with God because it demonstrates a lack of submission and foolishly attempts to take the recognition that is due to God alone. Believers need to be on constant guard against pride. The remedy for pride is humility. Humility is accompanied by wisdom rather than foolishness and keeps us on a path of revering the Lord (11:2). As Christ-followers we must always remember God is the only one worthy of constant praise and recognition. It is our purpose to bring glory to Him and not ourselves.

Father, I confess the sin of pride in my life, and I ask for Your forgiveness. I pray that I will remember that I am on earth to bring glory to You and not to call attention to myself. I ask that You will increase my humility and wisdom and that I will live with extreme reverence for You. I pray You will empower me to bring You glory all the days of my life.

In what areas of your life does pride rear its head? What are the dangers of pride? How do the Scriptures redirect our thoughts back to the glory of God and the praise that is due to Him? Practically speaking, what are ways you can guard against pride in your life?

Get All the Advice You Can

For lack of guidance a nation falls,
  but victory is won through many advisers.
—*Proverbs 11:14*

O ne of the key themes in the book of Proverbs is that we can't make it through life successfully without the help of others. It's with good reason that presidents have a cabinet, businesses and organizations have a board of directors, and churches have elders. No one individual has enough wisdom to make all of his or her own decisions and get them right all the time.[30] Proverbs 15:22 says, "Plans fail for lack of counsel, but with many advisers they succeed." All of us need input from other people to make right decisions.

Bad decisions from government officials can quickly cause international mayhem. For a nation to thrive, it's essential for leaders to seek advice from multiple sources. Solomon wrote, "For lack of guidance a nation falls" (11:14). In this context, the word used for "guidance" can serve as a nautical term and refer to the steering of a ship.[31] If no one is steering the ship or if a leader steers the ship in the wrong direction, it will soon be in an undesirable territory. To avoid moving in the wrong direction, a wise leader consults many advisors.

Obviously, if a leader is tasked with the decision of going to war or attempting to avoid it, many counselors are needed for such a decision. It is not uncommon for the book of Proverbs to speak of kings, so the references to war should be taken literally.[32] Proverbs 20:18 says, "Plans are established by seeking advice; so if you wage war, obtain guidance." Jesus communicated a similar concept in Luke 14:31–32: "Or suppose a king is about to go to war against another king. Won't he first sit down and consider whether he is able with ten thousand men to oppose the one coming against him with twenty thousand? If he is not able, he will send a delegation while the other is still a long way off and will ask for terms of peace."

Father, I pray You will surround me with wise people who will tell me the truth. Make me quick to seek the advice of others when I need it. Give me a humble spirit that can receive godly correction and make the necessary changes to make wise decisions.

Both on a national level and on a personal level, getting good advice can make the difference between success and failure. We all have blind spots that prevent us from seeing the full picture. Multiple advisors will cover the places we can't see properly. Sensible people take different perspectives into account and seek to learn from people with whom they might be prone to disagree. We can't wait for advisors to find us. Instead, we need to seek them out when we need them.

Speech and the Value of Self-Control

Fools show their annoyance at once,
  but the prudent overlook an insult.
—*Proverbs 12:16*

Read Proverbs 12

Social media has created a space where everyone has the opportunity to share thoughts on a public platform. Although there is value in this, it has produced a culture of outrage where people often say things online that they wouldn't say in person. Name-calling, insults, and verbal barbs are commonplace. Rather than ignoring rude remarks, there is a temptation to respond in a way that escalates the dialogue. The book of Proverbs has a lot to say about our words.

Solomon wrote that a fool lacks restraint and is quick to retaliate when confronted with a real or imagined insult.[33] A short temper escalates conflict in situations that could've been easily reconciled. In contrast, the prudent person is quick to overlook an offense. He ignores an insult and may even respond kindly. A wise person can avoid fights because he is patient and not easily offended. Proverbs 14:29 says, "Whoever is patient has great understanding, but one who is quick-tempered displays folly." A quick-tempered person might think he is defending his dignity, but his lack of self-control puts his foolishness on public display.

For better or worse, words are powerful. Solomon wrote, "The words of the reckless pierce like swords, but the tongue of the wise brings healing" (Proverbs 12:18). Our words have the potential to do either enormous damage or a significant amount of good. While they may not intend to, foolish people hurt others when they speak without restraint and do not give any thought to potential consequences. When a person is tempted to gossip or talk poorly about another human being, it reveals a lack of judgment.

A wise person chooses his words carefully. He knows that once words are spoken, they can be apologized for, but they can't be erased. All of us suffer from worry at times. Prolonged anxiety can lead us into a state of depression. But a kind word has the power to give someone who is struggling the encouragement to carry on. "Anxiety weighs down the heart, but a kind word cheers it up" (v. 25).

Father, I thank You for the gift of communication. Help me to speak words that heal and avoid saying anything that could harm. Help me to be quick to show restraint when I'm tempted to be easily angered. I ask for an attitude that helps me assume the best in other people.

It's likely that all of us will continue to communicate multiple times every day for the rest of our lives. Over the course of a lifetime, we will speak a countless number of words. Do your words bring healing or harm? Are you quick to anger and easily offended, or are you able to let things go? Whom do you know who is weighed down by the anxieties of life? Do you have an encouraging word that might help?

Choosing Words Carefully

From the fruit of their lips people enjoy good things,
    but the unfaithful have an appetite for violence.
Those who guard their lips preserve their lives,
    but those who speak rashly will come to ruin.
—*Proverbs 13:2–3*

Being a good listener is a quality that adds depth to our relationships. Unfortunately, many of us don't communicate with the goal of listening and learning. Too often, when someone else is speaking, we aren't listening but are thinking of what we will say next. The book of Proverbs teaches us to choose our words carefully. The goal isn't to speak just for the sake of talking. There is a time to speak words of wisdom, and there is a time to remain quiet.

Solomon taught that our speech has consequences. When Solomon wrote about "the fruit of their lips," he was referring to the fact that words influence results (v. 2). Words have the potential to bring a bounty of good things. Words can establish relationships, cast vision for the future, plant hope, and encourage the weary. Helpful words produce blessing.[34] In the same way, words can bring about good; they also have the potential to destroy. As Solomon pointed out, "The unfaithful have an appetite for violence" (v. 2). The Hebrew word for "appetite" is *nephesh* and is usually translated as "soul" or "deep-seated craving."[35] Words spoken by the unfaithful might be intended to inflict harm, or they may be expressed carelessly and unintentionally cause damage. One of the primary ways to distinguish a righteous person from an evil one is to listen to him speak.

We also need wisdom to know when to remain quiet. A wise person is comfortable with silence. He or she uses discretion in sharing information. Solomon wrote, "Those who guard their lips preserve their lives, but those who speak rashly will come to ruin" (v. 3). Foolish people tell everything they know without considering long-term consequences. It's unwise to quickly make promises you may not be able to keep, share private information, and offend others with poorly chosen words. Foolish people have a hard time being quiet, but constant talking reveals the hollowness of their character. Wise people listen more than they speak.

Father, I pray for discernment to know when to speak up and when to remain quiet. Help me to be a good listener. When I do speak, help me to say only words that bring life, hope, and healing. I pray I will never speak words that bring harm.

The book of James says, "My dear brothers and sisters, take note of this: Everyone should be quick to listen, slow to speak, and slow to become angry, because human anger does not produce the righteousness that God desires" (1:19–20). There are times when the wisest thing we can do is to say nothing at all.

Reason to Hope

Hope deferred makes the heart sick,
 but a longing fulfilled is a tree of life.
—*Proverbs 13:12*

Read Proverbs 13:12-25

H uman beings need hope to survive. As Solomon pointed out, we suffer greatly even when our hopes are delayed (v. 12). Hope "deferred" refers to a season when a promise is unfulfilled for an extended time. All of us go through times when it seems God is slow in answering our prayers. Our hearts can become sick with disappointment if we fail to remember that regardless of the time frame, God is faithful to keep His promises.

Many of us wrongly assume that "hope" is passive, meaning we assume the secular definition of hope. In a secular sense, hope can be described as simply wanting something to happen. For instance, you might hope for sunny weather during your vacation. You've probably heard someone say, "I'm h oping for the best." It's a passive attitude with no real expectations.

Biblical hope differs from secular hope in the sense that it is filled with active anticipation. The *Holman Bible Dictionary* defines biblical hope as "trustful expectation, particularly with reference to the fulfillment of God's promises. Biblical hope is the anticipation of a favorable outcome under God's guidance. More specifically, hope is the confidence that what God has done for us in the past guarantees our participation in what God will do in the future."[36] Biblical hope is a game changer.

On occasion, we will find ourselves in a season when we are forced to wait for something important and our hope might run low. As we wait, it's wise for us to redirect our thoughts to the promises of God and place our hope in His faithfulness. Hope is a central theme in the Christian faith. We serve the God of hope (Romans 15:13), we are called to hope (Ephesians 1:18), we are commanded to hold fast to our hope (Hebrews 10:23), and we are born again to a living hope (1 Peter 1:3).

As Christ-followers, we know God is who He says He is and there is nothing too hard for Him (Jeremiah 32:17). There is no situation beyond His reach (Isaiah 59:1). He can do more in a millisecond than a panel of the world's leaders can bring to pass in a lifetime. It doesn't matter if the issue is societal or personal. Regardless of what we are up against, we can move forward in hope.

Father, I thank You that You are faithful to keep Your promises. I ask that You will help me fix my eyes on all the ways that You keep Your promises. Help me to abound in hope. I pray You will increase my hope and faith as I wait to see Your promises come to pass in my life.

In this season of life, how would you describe your level of hope? What stirs your hope? As you survey your circumstances, what promises from the Scriptures can you study and meditate on to increase your hope?

Don't Be Your Own Worst Enemy

The wise woman builds her house,
　　but with her own hands the foolish one tears hers
　　down.
—*Proverbs 14:1*

Read Proverbs 14:1–19

Y ou've probably heard it said, "She's her own worst enemy."
The saying communicates that a person's own foolish choices
bring her problems that cause trouble. According to the Scriptures,
God established three distinct institutions: marriage and the
home (Genesis 2:18–25), government (Genesis 9:1–6; Romans 13),
and the local church (Acts 2).[37] A woman has tremendous influence in her home. Solomon pointed out that a woman can build
up her home or tear it down. It's often been said that the woman
sets the tone for the entire household. A wise woman will create
an atmosphere that gives everyone who lives there an opportunity to flourish, while a foolish woman lives in a way that creates a
toxic environment that causes things to deteriorate. Having good
relationships with the family members with whom we share our
homes is a central part of enjoying our lives.

Solomon's wives were his downfall. God's plan for marriage
included monogamy, but Solomon had seven hundred wives and
three hundred concubines (1 Kings 11:3). Some of Solomon's wives
were from pagan nations that didn't worship the living God of
the Bible. His pagan wives eventually influenced Solomon, and
he sinned against God and was disciplined by the Lord. Solomon
could say from bitter experience that wives either build up their

101

homes or tear them down (Proverbs 14:1). Wives who revere the Lord build healthy homes. Those who rebel against God create dysfunctional environments for their husbands and children.

A woman's character dramatically impacts her husband. Solomon wrote, "A wife of noble character is her husband's crown, but a disgraceful wife is like decay in his bones" (12:4). Obviously, there's an enormous difference between a "crown" and "decay," but those are the metaphors Solomon used to describe the potential influence a woman has on her husband.

None of us want to be our own worst enemy, especially in our home life. The book of Proverbs provides the most excellent instruction on relationship skills because it was given to us by God, and it provides the information we need to know to have healthy relationships in our marriage, family, jobs, and broader circles of influence. As we learn about God's wisdom and obey His instruction, our relationships will improve because we will mature in our people skills. The more we grow in our relationship with Christ, the greater capacity we will have to love other people well and make healthy decisions for our homes.

Father, thank You for my loved ones. I pray I will be someone who builds up my home rather than one who tears it down. Teach me to help my loved ones flourish and empower me to create a home life where my family members thrive.

Have you ever considered that you are either actively building up your home or tearing it down? Practically speaking, what are things you can do to create a loving and safe environment in your home? How can you help your family members flourish? If you are married, how would your husband and children describe the atmosphere in your home?

A Heart Tender to the Poor

Whoever oppresses the poor shows contempt for
their Maker,
but whoever is kind to the needy honors God.
—*Proverbs 14:31*

Read Proverbs 14:20–35

G od's people are called to care about the same things God does. The Bible makes it clear that God cares for the poor and oppressed. People who live in poverty are vulnerable to those in positions of power and lack the resources to fight injustices against them. God commits to protecting the oppressed, and He opposes those who take advantage of the vulnerable.

When people are unkind to the poor, God takes it personally. Solomon went as far as to say, "Whoever oppresses the poor shows contempt for their Maker" (v. 31). To oppress the poor means to "denigrate the significance, worth, and ability of someone or something."[38] In American culture, people often assign value or worth to other people based on their social status, possessions, connections, and degree of wealth. But this is an inaccurate barometer. All people have value because we are all created in God's image, including the poor (Genesis 1:27). Our possessions or lack of them don't give us value. God does. The poor and needy have an elevated status along with all of humanity because of their Creator. To oppress the poor is equivalent to showing contempt to the God who created them.

On the other hand, Solomon wrote, "But whoever is kind to the needy honors God" (Proverbs 14:31). In the ancient world, the "needy" were virtually destitute and depended on other people for their survival.[39] Some people are prone to look down on those who for reasons beyond their control can't provide for themselves. Solomon wrote, "The poor are shunned even by their neighbors, but the rich have many friends. It is a sin to despise one's neighbor, but blessed is the one who is kind to the needy" (vv. 20–21). When we are kind to the needy, we give honor to God. Those who oppress the poor will not go unpunished, and those who are kind to the poor will not go without reward.

Father, I pray You will give me a heart and mind that cares about the same things You do. Your Word makes it clear You care about the poor. I pray I will be quick to speak up for those who can't advocate for themselves. I ask You to give me opportunities to be generous with my resources. I pray that You will give me a heart that is tender to the poor.

Apart from Christ, we are all spiritually destitute. How we treat the poor and oppressed serves as an indicator of how well we understand what God has done for us in the finished work of Jesus Christ (Romans 5:8). What is your attitude toward the poor and oppressed? Do you ignore them or look down on them? Do you realize they are people in need who are created in the image of God? Are you willing to help those who lack essential resources to survive?

Responding Well

A gentle answer turns away wrath,
  but a harsh word stirs up anger.
The tongue of the wise adorns knowledge,
  but the mouth of the fool gushes folly.
—*Proverbs 15:1–2*

I t's been said, "If two people agree on everything, only one person is thinking." Disagreements with other people are bound to come, but how we react will influence the outcome. Our words have the potential to escalate conflicts or defuse them. When we are verbally attacked or spoken to with harsh language, there's a temptation to respond in the same manner. Instinctually, human beings are prone to act defensively when we are the object of another person's wrath. But doing so increases tension.

When Solomon wrote, "A gentle answer turns away wrath, but a harsh word stirs up anger" (v. 1), he wasn't suggesting we should go along with something we disagree with or give in to every argument. Instead, he was saying the tone of our voice and the way we approach the conversation has the potential to defuse the situation and make it much easier to settle the matter peacefully.[40] Communication doesn't only consist of words. It includes the way we deliver our words. In the midst of a disagreement, wise people avoid sarcasm, eye-rolling, or anything that shows contempt for the other person. Addressing another person with respect, a gentle tone, and an amicable attitude will go a long way toward a peaceful resolution.

In contrast, Solomon wrote that "the mouth of the fool gushes folly" (v. 2). In other words, a fool says everything that comes to mind and disregards potential consequences. When a fool is angry, he or she communicates with insults, sarcasm, cut downs, and other nonverbal modes of communication that do nothing but escalate tension. Once again, it's a matter of the heart. Jesus said, "A good man brings good things out of the good stored up in his heart, and an evil man brings evil things out of the evil stored up in his heart. For the mouth speaks what the heart is full of" (Luke 6:45).

Worldly wisdom instructs us to fight for our rights and win an argument at any cost. Godly wisdom teaches us to communicate in a way that leads to a win-win situation that strengthens the "unity of the Spirit through the bond of peace" (Ephesians 4:3).[41] Our natural inclination might be to respond to wrath with wrath. But wisdom teaches us to react with an intentionality that reflects the fruit of the Spirit (Galatians 5:22–23).

Father, I pray that when I'm confronted with anger or wrath, I will respond with amicability. I ask that You will help me be assertive and communicate in a way that explains my thoughts without escalating the situation or disrespecting those with whom I disagree. I pray that You will make me an excellent communicator.

How do you respond when someone confronts you in an angry tone? Are you prone to be defensive? Do you shrink back in fear? When we are wise in our speech, we can assert ourselves in a way that communicates our thoughts and desires without escalating the situation. Godly wisdom has the potential to make us excellent communicators.

God Is Aware of Our Motives

To humans belong the plans of the heart,
>   but from the LORD comes the proper answer of
>   the tongue.
All a person's ways seem pure to them,
>   but motives are weighed by the LORD.
Commit to the LORD whatever you do,
>   and he will establish your plans.

—Proverbs 16:1–3

How many times have you made plans without seeking God and then asked Him to bless them? It's a common trap we've all fallen into on occasion. The opening verses of Proverbs 16 speak to God's control over events. God is sovereign over every facet of our lives, including the areas we think we control. It's wise for us to make plans prayerfully, and the Bible teaches us to do so (James 4:13–15), but we must remember that ultimately God will determine whether or not our plans succeed.[42]

When we make plans, we usually believe we are making the right decision (Proverbs 16:2). But God weighs both our actions and our motives. It's possible to do a good thing with a wrong motive. As sinners, we are prone to deceive ourselves about our own goodness. If judgment were our responsibility, we'd find ourselves innocent. Generally, we compare ourselves to other people, and if we seem to be doing better than they are, we feel good about ourselves. But God doesn't compare our righteousness to that of others. God judges us compared to His righteous standard and even knows the hidden places of our hearts (1 Corinthians 4:4–5). Our motives are no secret to God.[43]

Rather than making our own plans and asking God to bless them, Solomon instructed his readers in another way. Proverbs 16:3

says, "Commit to the LORD whatever you do, and he will establish your plans." Practically speaking, this means we are to pray as we make plans and allow God's Word to be the ultimate guide. At that point we can move forward and work our plan with diligence, submitting all of it to the Lord. It's important to realize that even when our plans don't work out as we wanted, God can use what happened for our good in ways we may not be able to see (Romans 8:28). Knowing God is in control of every aspect of our lives allows us to seek Him prayerfully as we plan, do our best work, and then trust the outcome to Him.

Father, I pray I will be wise in my planning and seek You through prayer and the study of Your Word before I make plans. Teach me to rest in Your sovereign will for my life. Lead me into a relationship with You where I trust You completely and know with confidence that whatever happens will be for my good and Your glory.

Are there specific areas of your life in which you need to seek God's guidance? Does knowing that God is in control of every aspect of your life give you peace or does it make you anxious? How would prayerfully seeking His guidance and then moving forward in faith allow you to live with certainty that you are in the center of His perfect will?

Speak Words That Heal

The hearts of the wise make their mouths prudent,
  and their lips promote instruction.
Gracious words are a honeycomb,
  sweet to the soul and healing to the bones.
—*Proverbs 16:23–24*

Read Proverbs 16:16-33

Children say cruel things to each other. Very few of us escape our school years without getting our feelings hurt over something another child said to us. Often as children, we were taught to respond to a verbal barb by saying, "Sticks and stones may break my bones, but words will never hurt me." Of course, that old saying is not true. Words wound us deeply. There's a good chance you remember a time from years ago when someone spoke unkind words to you. Harsh words from a parent, teacher, or friend can linger for decades. That's why wise people choose their words carefully.

Solomon wrote that wise people are prudent with their words (v. 23), which means they show good judgment in their speech. As a result, their words help rather than hurt, and listening to individuals such as these motivates us to learn and embrace what is said. Foolish people give no thought to what they say, and their words cause damage. On the other hand, Solomon wrote, "Gracious words are a honeycomb, sweet to the soul and healing to the bones" (v. 24).

It's astounding to realize that our words have the potential to bring healing. In the ancient world, honey was the sweetest substance available, and Solomon was intentional with his imagery.[44]

Not only are kind words sweet to the soul, but they have the potential to have a healing effect on the body. Most of us expect anything medicinal to be bitter in taste and sweets to be harmful, but kind words are both sweet and health-giving.[45] The apostle Paul offered instruction to the church at Ephesus on how a Christ-follower is supposed to speak: "Do not let any unwholesome talk come out of your mouths, but only what is helpful for building others up according to their needs, that it may benefit those who listen" (Ephesians 4:29). It's easy for us to forget the impact our words have on other people. We have the potential to speak words that help or hurt, maim or heal. We need wisdom to choose our words wisely.

Father, thank You for the privilege we have to communicate with each other. I pray You will quickly convict me when I am out of line in my speech. Help me to speak words that are a benefit to those who hear. I pray I will routinely speak words of kindness and that my words will never harm.

Have you ever been on the receiving end of unkind words? How do those experiences influence your speech? Whom do you know that could benefit from a kind word from you today? How can you use your words to bring healing to someone who is hurting?

Love Covers an Offense

Whoever would foster love covers over an offense,
but whoever repeats the matter separates close
friends.

—*Proverbs 17:9*

Read Proverbs 17

W hen someone commits an offense against us, our first inclination is to tell other people. We want others to know about our offender's poor behavior and the injustice we've suffered. As a result, there's a temptation to fall into the trap of gossip and complaint. The Bible repeatedly warns about the sins of our mouth. The book of Proverbs offers another option. Rather than resorting to gossip, we can choose to remain silent about the issue. Solomon identified this as a way we foster love (v. 9).

Gossips get negative publicity in the New Testament (Romans 1:29; 2 Corinthians 12:20). Some people believe that to gossip means to share information that isn't true, and therefore, if what they are saying is true, it's not classified as gossip. That's an incorrect assessment. Gossip includes repeating information that has the potential to embarrass someone, sharing personal information that doesn't need to be publicly known, or spreading lies and falsehoods.

The book of James has strong words for those who don't guard their tongues: "With the tongue we praise our Lord and Father, and with it we curse human beings, who have been made in God's likeness. Out of the same mouth come praise and cursing. My brothers and sisters, this should not be" (3:9–10).

Gossip creates a toxic environment and reflects poorly on those who participate. Solomon went as far as to warn his readers to stay away from people who gossip (Proverbs 20:19). When someone sins against us, the wise thing to do is remain silent. Repeating a matter has the potential to separate close friends (Proverbs 17:9). Blaise Pascal said, "Few friendships would endure if each knew what his friend said of him in his absence."[46] An excellent boundary to keep is to resolve not to say anything behind a person's back that you wouldn't say in his or her presence.

It's easy to say we'll quit gossiping, but we can't do it without God's help. James 3:8 says, "No human being can tame the tongue. It is a restless evil, full of deadly poison." Even though we can't tame our tongues, it doesn't mean that God can't change us. What's impossible for human beings is possible with God (Luke 18:27).

Father, when others treat me poorly, I pray You will help me to respond in love by not gossiping about the event. I pray I will avoid gossip and not participate when I hear it. Help me be someone who only speaks words that are helpful.

Gossip is rampant. Are you inclined to gather around the watercooler at work to listen to the latest scoop on your coworkers? Are you tempted to repeat an offense when someone treats you poorly? Do you find it difficult to keep from sharing information you know other people would find interesting? Our words are powerful. They have the potential to heal or destroy. Let's ask God's help in choosing them wisely.

Characteristics of a Fool

An unfriendly person pursues selfish ends
    and against all sound judgment starts quarrels.
Fools find no pleasure in understanding
    but delight in airing their own opinions.
When wickedness comes, so does contempt,
    and with shame comes reproach.
—*Proverbs 18:1–3*

N o one wants to be a fool, but there's a good chance you know a few. In the book of Proverbs, a fool is someone who lacks wisdom, and "find[s] no pleasure in understanding" (v. 2). Proverbs 18 contains multiple descriptions of a fool, and you will find three in verses 1–3 alone.

First, a fool is someone who isolates himself from others (v. 1). He tends to be antisocial and might be regarded as a loner who is self-centered.[47] As a result of his self-absorption, he disregards the counsel of others because he thinks he knows best. If someone tries to talk some sense into him, he "against all sound judgment starts quarrels" (v. 1). A fool often responds to wisdom with insults, contempt, and a defensive attitude. If you communicate with a fool, he often twists the conversation, and his line of thinking is difficult to follow. Conversations with a fool often escalate to arguments, and disagreements end badly.

Second, a fool is opinionated (v. 2). When a fool communicates he doesn't do so with the goal of gaining new information or learning something, because "fools find no pleasure in understanding" (v. 2). Instead, a fool only wants to air his own opinions while he seeks to ignore, disregard, or scoff at those whose views differ from his. A fool believes that everyone should think the way he does. If you disagree with a fool, he will assume you are wrong. Fools seldom change their minds and refuse to contemplate an issue from another person's point of view.

Third, because of their lack of wisdom, fools will humiliate themselves. A lifestyle of isolation, refusing to listen, and talking too much takes its toll. It's difficult to maintain a relationship with fools because they aren't enjoyable to be around. On occasion, foolishness leads to a wicked lifestyle (v. 3). With wickedness come contempt, shame, and reproach.

Proverbs 18 has much to say about the characteristics of a fool. The anecdote to foolishness is wisdom, and wisdom comes through a relationship with Jesus Christ. Jesus is the embodiment of the wisdom of God (1 Corinthians 1:30). A fool has no wisdom, but Jesus is the source of all grace and truth (John 1:14).

Father, I pray You will give me wisdom when communicating with a fool. I also ask that if I have any foolish tendencies, You will increase my wisdom. I pray I will be someone who seeks out wise counsel, heeds godly instruction, and makes a habit of listening with the intention to learn.

Are you receptive to the counsel of others? Are you more inclined to talk or to listen? How do you respond when you receive instruction?

Don't Speak the Enemy's Language

A false witness will not go unpunished,
and whoever pours out lies will not go free.
—*Proverbs 19:5*

Read Proverbs 19

A couple of the first lessons we learn as children are never to tell a lie and always tell the truth. But in our fallen nature, all of us have been tempted to lie to avoid getting in trouble or to prevent disappointing someone. But lies come with consequences. The Bible teaches that God is a God of absolute truth and He detests lying (Proverbs 6:16–17). While it may seem that falsehood is the only way to prevent being backed into a corner, a lying tongue is not a permanent solution to the problem. Solomon wrote, "Truthful lips endure forever, but a lying tongue lasts only a moment" (Proverbs 12:19).

God's people should avoid lies because God hates falsehood. When we tell a lie, we are speaking the Enemy's language. When Jesus addressed a group of nonbelievers who questioned His identity, He said, "You belong to your father, the devil, and you want to carry out your father's desires. He was a murderer from the beginning, not holding to the truth, for there is no truth in him. When he lies, he speaks his native language, for he is a liar and the father of lies" (John 8:44).

The Bible makes it clear that lies have consequences. In the Old Testament, there was a strict penalty for perjury (Deuteronomy 19:18–21), but it wasn't always enforced.[48] These verses warn that

God will always judge sin even if a court of law allows a false witness to go unpunished. People who habitually tell falsehoods will soon earn a reputation as a liar. Lying is detrimental to relationships because all relationships are built on trust. For obvious reasons, it's impossible to trust a liar. A lifestyle of lying will lead to broken relationships and a destroyed reputation that may take years to rebuild.

Rather than telling a lie, in the long run it's easier to tell the truth and immediately deal with the potential fallout. A person who tells the truth regardless of the consequences may have some uncomfortable conversations, but will soon build a reputation of solid character. Perhaps you've heard the old cliché, "I'd rather someone hurt me with the truth than comfort me with a lie." Regardless of the situation, all people hate being lied to.

Father, Your Word makes it clear that You hate lying, and I don't want to participate in any behavior that offends You. I pray You will be quick to convict me when I'm tempted to speak a lie. Empower me to speak words of truth regardless of the consequences.

When you find yourself in a difficult situation, are you tempted to react by telling a lie? Have you ever thought a "little white lie" never hurt anyone? Are you prone to mislead or exaggerate? Have you ever told the truth and suffered the consequences of honesty?

Resisting the Urge to Retaliate

Do not say, "I'll pay you back for this wrong!"
Wait for the Lord, and he will avenge you.
—*Proverbs 20:22*

Read Proverbs 20

For most people, it's instinctual to want to pay back someone who has caused us harm. If another person has caused damage to you or your family, it creates justified anger that longs for swift justice. But Proverbs warns against retaliation. Instead, God's people are to wait for the Lord to deal with the matter.[49] When we retaliate, we place ourselves in the position of judge and jury. This is a mistake, because only God has that authority.

Waiting for justice to be done is difficult. As we wait for God to deal with our offenders, it's wise to remember that God is a God of justice. All sins we commit and those committed against us will be addressed. Every sin ever committed either will be covered by the blood of Christ or will separate the offender from God for eternity. As Christ-followers, we must trust God to deal with our offenders. This is easier said than done, especially if the sin committed against us was particularly grievous.

We all know or have heard of people who've had heinous crimes committed against them by the hands of offenders who don't show an ounce of remorse. But in God's wisdom, He knows the burden of retaliation is too much for us to bear. As Christ-followers we have to set our desire to retaliate at the foot of the cross and trust that God will deal with it in due time. Dealing with sin is not our job; it's God's. Paul wrote in Romans 12:19, "Do not take revenge, my dear friends, but leave room for God's wrath, for it is written: 'It is mine to avenge; I will repay,' says the Lord."

Although it's tempting to believe retaliating against our offender will make us feel better, the truth is it won't. In fact, retaliating has the potential to make us more like our offender. In some cultures, people have resorted to murder to avenge themselves against wrongs committed against them or their family. Other times revenge takes place in a courtroom, where people have been known to give false testimony about someone who mistreated them. As Christ-followers, we don't have the option of participating in evil, even if someone has done evil to us.[50]

Father, I know You are a God of justice. Help me to trust You to deal with my offenders. When I'm tempted to retaliate, I pray You will empower me to resist. I thank You that You are able and willing to deal with my offenders. I pray You will teach me to trust You to do so as You see fit.

What is your initial response when someone sins against you? Do you fantasize about how you might get back at that person? Do you find it difficult to trust God to deal with your offenders? Do you believe God is just and will deal with all offenses?

God Is Sovereign Over All

> In the Lᴏʀᴅ's hand the king's heart is a stream of
> water
> that he channels toward all who please him.
> —*Proverbs 21:1*

Read Proverbs 21

S olomon was king when the book of Proverbs was written. In his era, Solomon was the prime example of leadership, so it's not surprising he included multiple proverbs that address leadership and running the government.[51] Solomon understood that life in a high position of leadership came with privileges few people possess. A leader of Solomon's stature lived in the public eye, and there was significant recognition that came with his position. Citizens went to extreme lengths to show reverence to the king. When one person holds a great deal of power and influence, it's easy to believe he or she is unstoppable. At a glance, it sometimes seems influential leaders aren't accountable to anyone, but that's not true.

Solomon understood there's a greater authority than even the world's most powerful leaders. He wrote, "In the LORD's hand the king's heart is a stream of water that he channels toward all who please him" (v. 1). God's authority extends over the lives of the most influential people on the planet in the same way it reigns over ordinary citizens. Although it might seem that the world's most powerful leaders make decisions unhindered by anyone, God is still on the throne. God is in control of history, and He uses rulers to carry out His plan for the nations.[52] In the same way that a farmer directs water into an irrigation ditch and waters the field of his choice, so God directs the heart of every king (v. 1).

Even the world's most powerful rulers have limited authority. God rules over all things, including the heart and mind of the king. In the Old Testament, there is a vivid picture of what happened to King Saul when David was anointed king. "Now the Spirit of the LORD had departed from Saul, and an evil spirit from the LORD tormented him" (1 Samuel 16:14). Some people have misinterpreted this verse to suggest it means an individual can lose his or her salvation, but that isn't what this text addresses. Instead, it demonstrates God's sovereignty over who possesses the Spirit's empowering for a specific role.[53] God rules every aspect of life, including those in a position of power and esteem.

Father, I thank You that You are in total control of all things and all people. I pray those in positions of leadership will submit to Your lordship and lead with Your wisdom. Help me to rest in Your sovereignty and to be mindful that You are in control and are faithful.

Are you mindful of the fact that God's sovereignty reaches even to those who are nonbelievers? Are you more inclined to complain about your elected officials or to pray for them to submit to Christ's lordship? Does God's sovereignty over your life put you at ease?

Materialism Is a Spiritual Issue

The rich rule over the poor,
   and the borrower is slave to the lender.
—*Proverbs 22:7*

Read Proverbs 22:1–16

Benjamin Franklin said, "Money never made a man happy yet, nor will it. There is nothing in its nature to produce happiness. The more a man has, the more he wants. Instead of its filling a vacuum, it makes one. If it satisfies one want, it doubles and triples that want another way."[54]

Although the United States is the most prosperous nation in the world, many Americans are swimming in debt. Proverbs warns about excessive debt because of potential consequences. Solomon said, "The rich rule over the poor, and the borrower is slave to the lender" (v. 7). Wealthy people and organizations often have power over the poor, who have no resources to dispute the authority of those who oppress them. Poverty leads to a cycle of debt, which places the poor in a deeper bind. In the same say, a borrower is a slave to the lender. This is always true in an emotional sense, but in the Old Testament, it could be true in the literal sense (2 Kings 4:1).[55]

Working hard to provide the necessities of life is an excellent virtue. But working to the point of exhaustion to pay for things you don't need is foolish. Excessive debt eliminates choices in regard to vocation. How many people do you know who would rather be in a different line of work but are forced to stay in jobs they hate because they need a higher salary? When you are tethered to a specific wage and you expend all your energy in the pursuit of materialism, you are forced to sacrifice other goals that are more important and longer lasting.

Materialistic possessions can and will vanish in an instant. That's why Jesus said, "Do not store up for yourselves treasures on earth, where moths and vermin destroy, and where thieves break in and steal. But store up for yourselves treasures in heaven, where moths and vermin do not destroy, and where thieves do not break in and steal. For where your treasure is, there your heart will be also" (Matthew 6:19–21).

Obviously, it takes money to live. But Christ-followers must not fall into the trap of living for money. At its core, materialism is a spiritual issue. People are searching for awe in possessions that they will only find in a relationship with God. Money is neither good nor evil, but when we pursue money more than we do God, it becomes an idol.

Father, I thank You for providing the material resources I need to live comfortably. I pray You will be quick to convict me when I step over the line into materialism. Help me to view my possessions with proper perspective and remember that lasting satisfaction can only be found in You.

Do you earn money to live or do you live for money? Are you prone to overspend when you are feeling down? Do you search for your identity in your possessions rather than in your relationship with God?

Choose Your Friends Wisely

Do not make friends with a hot-tempered person,
    do not associate with one easily angered,
or you may learn their ways,
    and get yourself ensnared.
—*Proverbs 22:24–25*

On occasion, all of us become angry. But there's a difference between someone who is occasionally angered and someone who is habitually outraged. In Hebrew, a "hot-tempered person" (v. 24) literally means a "possessor of anger" or a "lord of rage." Similarly, one who is "easily angered" (v. 24) is described as a "man of wrath."[56] The book of Proverbs warns us not to make friends with people who are chronically angry because it's possible we will develop a similar problem with anger.

Motivational speaker Jim Rohn said we are the average of the five people with whom we spend the most time.[57] While this may or may not be true, there's no doubt that our closest relationships influence our behavior, thinking, and decisions. Friendships have the potential to be a negative influence, but positive relationships make us stronger. Solomon wrote, "As iron sharpens iron, so one person sharpens another" (Proverbs 27:17). In the same way that a file sharpens an ax, good friends encourage one another to grow. Sometimes growth requires painful feedback from our friends that we'd rather not hear, but a good friend won't hesitate to tell us the truth if it will ultimately help us.

God hasn't called any of us to be spiritual loners. We need godly friends in our life. You can scour the Scriptures from Genesis to Revelation, and you won't find a single instance of a man or woman in the Bible who encouraged anyone to "go it alone." Life is too hard, and the Enemy is too fierce. Peter wrote, "Be alert and of sober mind. Your enemy the devil prowls around like a roaring lion looking for someone to devour. Resist him, standing firm in the faith, because you know that the family of believers throughout the world is undergoing the same kind of sufferings" (1 Peter 5:8–9). As Christ-followers we need one another's encouragement, counsel, and fellowship. Lone Christians are vulnerable.

No one is perfect, and therefore we'll never be or find the perfect friend. But Proverbs instructs us to avoid people who are easily angered and those who gossip. For better or worse, our friends will influence our lives. A big part of finding good friends is learning to be a good friend, and the book of Proverbs has much to teach us about maintaining healthy relationships. As we grow in wisdom, our relationships will be impacted positively, and our friendships will increase in number and depth.

Father, I thank You for the gift of friendship. I pray You will teach me to be an excellent friend to others. I ask You to bring godly people into my life and that I will enjoy healthy and authentic friendships.

How would you describe the quality of your friendships? Are you a good friend? Have you ever considered asking God to give you godly friends? What steps can you take to make new friends or deepen the friendships you already have?

When Things Aren't as They Seem

When you sit to dine with a ruler,
    note well what is before you,
and put a knife to your throat
    if you are given to gluttony.
Do not crave his delicacies
    for that food is deceptive.
Do not wear yourself out to get rich;
    do not trust your own cleverness.
—*Proverbs 23:1–4*

Read Proverbs 23

In a culture that thrives on ambition, climbing a social ladder is something many people pursue. The idea is to continually position yourself for promotions, gain a broader network of associates and colleagues, and be known among the most influential people in your field. Although a lot of this happens in the workplace, a great deal of social climbing happens off the clock at parties, golf outings, restaurants, and a variety of other events.

Solomon had advice for the social climber who had been invited to dinner at the home of an influential individual. He warned that hospitality can be deceptive. The point Solomon was making is that a wealthy host might use the luxuries he provides to coerce a less influential person to do his bidding.[58] When someone is trying to excel in a given field, it's easy to be awed by those who are already successful. Solomon warned the social climber to be careful. Influential people seldom do favors for no reason and often want something in return. It's foolish to be blinded by the luxuries of a lavish meal or an extravagant outing.[59]

Solomon was warning it was possible that the host could have ulterior motives that obligated the guests. When Solomon wrote, "Put a knife to your throat if you are given to gluttony," he was using hyperbole (v. 2). His point was to use cautious restraint, and if that's not possible, to abstain from what's offered. There are times that things aren't the way they seem. A lavish meal, an extravagant party, or a generous favor may come with strings attached.

Certainly, there's nothing wrong with working hard and wanting to be successful in your field of work. As people who are created in the image of God, we are designed to do our work with excellence. But if you are willing to forfeit your integrity or pursue success at the expense of your family, then the desire to climb the social ladder is problematic.

Father, I thank You for my work and the ways You have gifted me. I pray that I will use the skills You have given me to bring You glory. Give me the wisdom to know how to balance my desire for success and my desire to live with integrity. Teach me to work in a way that always gives You honor and glory.

How do you balance the desire for success and your integrity? Are you willing to go to any length to climb the social ladder, or do you have boundaries in regard to what you will and won't do?

God Disapproves of Gloating

Though the righteous fall seven times, they rise
again,
but the wicked stumble when calamity strikes.
Do not gloat when your enemy falls;
when they stumble, do not let your heart rejoice,
or the LORD will see and disapprove
and turn his wrath away from them.
—*Proverbs 24:16–18*

All of us experience difficult seasons in life. Both the righteous and the wicked fall, but when the righteous fall, they get up again because God sustains them. Although it might be tempting to celebrate when the wicked stumble, Proverbs warns against gloating of any kind. God is so opposed to this type of behavior that the text suggests He would rather turn away from the retribution of the wicked than to gaze upon gloating.[60] Gloating suggests an attitude of superiority that is rooted in pride. The Scriptures make it clear that God hates pride and that pride won't go unpunished (Proverbs 6:16–17; 16:5). It was the sin of pride that caused the fall of humanity (Genesis 3). Adam and Eve believed they knew more than God, and they paid a steep price for their disobedience.

Solomon wrote, "Pride goes before destruction, a haughty spirit before a fall" (Proverbs 16:18). Pride is both deceptive and dangerous. Prideful people assume they know what's best, and they refuse counsel from other people. To some degree, all people struggle with pride, but some more than others. A prideful person lacks humility and is therefore prone to boast when someone else stumbles. Pride always assumes a stance of superiority. Prideful people are inclined to sin with their mouths by exaggerating, slandering, gossiping, complaining, gloating, and boasting.

The anecdote to pride is humility. Above all else, all people need humility before God, which comes from fear, or reverence, for the Lord (Proverbs 22:4). It's impossible for someone to revere God above all things and to simultaneously be full of selfish pride. Among the key themes in Proverbs is to trust God rather than ourselves and to seek humility and resist pride. When we walk in humility before God and before others, we avoid many of the sins God hates. A humble person won't gloat when his enemy stumbles. The prophet Micah described this living beautifully: "He has shown you, O mortal, what is good. And what does the LORD require of you? To act justly and to love mercy and to walk humbly with your God" (Micah 6:8).

Father, Your Word makes it clear that You despise gloating and any behavior that is rooted in pride. I ask that You remove these flaws from my character and replace them with the fruits of the Spirit (Galatians 5:22–23). I pray I will walk humbly with You. Empower me to live in a way that brings honor to You.

Are you tempted to gloat when the wicked stumble? Do you see symptoms of pride in your life? How would you describe your attitude toward God and toward others? What would it look like for you to humble yourself before the Lord?

Avoiding the Road to Poverty

A little sleep, a little slumber,
    a little folding of the hands to rest—
and poverty will come on you like a thief
    and scarcity like an armed man.
—*Proverbs 24:33–34*

In the creation account, God modeled what our work life should look like when He labored for six days, and on the seventh day, He rested from His work (Genesis 2:2). God didn't need the rest because He neither sleeps nor slumbers, but He did so to set an example for us to follow (Psalm 121:4). The Scriptures make it clear that sleep is a welcome respite from labor. Undoubtedly, God wants His people to get adequate rest from work because He gave us the gift of a weekly Sabbath.

Sleep is necessary and good, but indulging in it to the point of laziness is wrong. Proverbs issues stern warnings to those who love sleep, because it's a path that leads to poverty. The author of Proverbs 24 told the story of passing a field that belonged to a sluggard (v. 30). Due to the man's laziness, he'd failed to work his land, and thorns and weeds were choking out the crops.[61] The man had failed to repair the stone wall surrounding his field, so animals were able to come in and destroy what little crops were coming up. As the writer pondered the scene, he concluded that the man's laziness would soon destroy the place. His poor work ethic would leave him as destitute as a victim of a robbery (vv. 33–34).

Our society keeps running because people get out of bed each morning whether they feel like it or not and do their part until the job is done. There is no value in a task that is only partially completed. Life depends on people who are willing to work until a job is finished. Some people are tempted to try to avoid work, but that's a dangerous trap. According to the Scriptures, hard work is the only way to prosperity. There are no shortcuts. The book of Proverbs warns that those who prefer to avoid work and sleep all day will come to poverty. Proverbs mentions the "sluggard" or the "slothful man" at least seventeen times, and nothing positive is ever mentioned regarding such a person. We need to remember that work is not a curse to be avoided. God gave Adam work to do in the garden before sin entered the world (Genesis 2:15).[62]

Father, I thank You for giving Your image bearers work to do. I ask that You will give me a balanced view of work and sleep. I pray You will help me to do my best work every day. I ask that You will help me let go of any lazy tendencies and give my full effort to the work You give me to do.

How would you describe your work ethic? What would your boss and coworkers say about the quality of your work? Do you attempt to avoid work or do you put in a full day's effort? What steps can you take to do your best work?

Being a Good Friend During Bad Times

Like one who takes away a garment on a cold day,
   or like vinegar poured on a wound,
   is one who sings songs to a heavy heart.
—*Proverbs 25:20*

Read Proverbs 25

J esus wasn't kidding when He said, "In this world you will have trouble" (John 16:33). Most of us know people dealing with health crises, relationship problems, depression and anxiety, unemployment, and a variety of other problems that plague the human race. But Jesus said in the latter half of John 16:33, "But take heart! I have overcome the world."

One of the ways we get through hard times is with the help of our friends and loved ones. When times are hard, we need more than well-meaning acquaintances who tell us to call if we need anything. But when a friend is suffering, it's sometimes difficult to know how to help. Proverbs warns us not to "[sing] songs to a heavy heart" (v. 20).

A positive attitude is a good thing, but it must be coupled with sensitivity. When a friend is suffering, it's tactless and insensitive to attempt to cheer him up and ignore the depth of his distress. Doing so will make him even more miserable, like one who takes a coat on a cold day, or pours vinegar on a wound (v. 20).[63] Most of us have experienced a time when we attempted to comfort someone and came up short. Common pitfalls include trying to explain why the season of adversity is happening, feeling the need to defend God for allowing the crises, and assuring the sufferer things will improve when in reality we have no idea whether they will or not.

In times of suffering, our friends need our presence more than our answers. It's not all that difficult to find a friend to laugh with, but finding one who will grieve with you is another story. Quietly sitting with a friend who is grieving is one of the most profound gifts we can offer someone. Most of the time words aren't necessary. When a friend is suffering, it's good to meet needs when we can. Paul wrote in Galatians 6:2, "Carry each other's burdens, and in this way you will fulfill the law of Christ." Delivering a meal or running an errand is far more helpful to someone in a season of distress than our opinion about why things happened the way they did.

Father, I thank You for the gift of friendship. I pray You will teach me to be a good friend in bad times. Give me discernment so I know how to help. I ask that You will make me the kind of friend others reach out to in their time of need and that I will be a good friend to all.

Do you struggle to know what to do when friends are suffering? Are you tempted to give them advice or offer an unsolicited opinion? What is helpful for you during seasons of adversity?

There Are No Shortcuts

A sluggard says, "There's a lion in the road,
   a fierce lion roaming the streets!"
As a door turns on its hinges,
   so a sluggard turns on his bed.
A sluggard buries his hand in the dish;
   he is too lazy to bring it back to his mouth.
—*Proverbs 26:13–15*

M illions of people each year are enticed by programs that promise maximum results with minimum effort. Whether it's a get-rich-quick scheme, the promise of rapid weight loss, or a workout plan that promises six-pack abs in thirty days, shortcuts are tempting. The problem is, there are no shortcuts. The book of Proverbs teaches that hard work is necessary for any endeavor to succeed. Still, some people go to extreme lengths to escape work. The Bible calls lazy people "sluggards."

A person who wants to avoid a task can usually come up with a reason to do so, even if the idea is cowardly. Solomon highlighted the far-fetched reasons lazy people come up with to keep from doing their work. In verse 13, Solomon depicted the sluggard as saying, "There's a lion in the road, a fierce lion roaming the streets!" Lions seldom came into town and therefore posed little threat. But the sluggard was willing to use any reason to postpone or dodge the job he was supposed to do.[64] In general "sluggards" or lazy people are irritating to employers because they inevitably fail to complete a task, or if they do finish, the work is shoddy at best. A sluggard takes every possible shortcut and pays no attention to the outcome.

Proverbs suggests the goal of a sluggard person is nothing more than sleep. Solomon described the lazy person this way: "As a door turns on its hinges, so a sluggard turns on his bed" (v. 14). Obviously, all human beings require sleep, and God provides sleep as a needed respite. But when someone spends too much time sleeping, he is wasting his day, and ultimately, if laziness turns into a lifestyle, he is wasting his life. All human beings have a limited time in this world, and we need to make the most of our days. Wisely, the psalmist prayed, "Teach us to number our days, that we may gain a heart of wisdom" (Psalm 90:12). Laziness that isn't dealt with only continues to get worse. Solomon used a tongue-in-cheek description of a lazy man who gets to the point that he is too lazy to feed himself (v. 15).

Father, I pray I will be someone who works hard each day. Increase my motivation to do excellent work. Help me to remember my time on earth is limited and I need to make the most of every day You give me.

Are you tempted to take shortcuts? How would you describe your work ethic? Are you motivated to do excellent work or do you do the bare minimum? There are no shortcuts to success. Hard work is required to enjoy good results in any area of life.

No Room for Bragging

Let someone else praise you, and not your own
mouth;
an outsider, and not your own lips.
—*Proverbs 27:2*

Read Proverbs 27

In modern times it's not uncommon for people to think they need to make a name for themselves. In past generations, humility and discreetness were valued as virtues, but in today's society the mind-set is, "If you don't blow your own horn, no one else will." The problem is, this attitude isn't biblical. In fact, it's a sin. In the New Testament, James instructed his readers, "Humble yourselves before the Lord, and he will lift you up" (James 4:10). As Christians, we aren't called to make a name for ourselves. We are called to bring attention to the name of Christ.

The book of Proverbs offers another way. Solomon wrote, "Let someone else praise you, and not your own mouth; an outsider, and not your own lips" (27:2). No one enjoys the company of a braggart. When we sing our own praises, we aren't drawing attention to God but attempting to bring glory to ourselves. Calling attention to our achievements is a sin that is motivated by pride because we want to be sure everyone else recognizes our ability and gives us due credit.[65] Obviously, there is nothing wrong with being commended for good work. But Solomon instructed that if there is real merit in something we've done, others will notice and give credit where it's due.

Seeking the praise of others will oftentimes lead to an unhealthy desire for adulation that has the potential to damage our relationship with God. In the gospel of John, such a thing happened to the Jews: "At the same time many even among the leaders believed in [Jesus]. But because of the Pharisees they would not openly acknowledge their faith for fear they would be put out of the synagogue, for they loved human praise more than praise from God" (12:42–43).

At the core of idolatry is loving something more than we love God. Boasting is not only obnoxious; it's dangerous because it can lead to a love of praise from others. When we put the praise of man, rather than God, at the center of our aspirations, we will lead a life of desperation. Human beings are fickle, and we will never keep other people satisfied for long. And even in the midst of human praise, we have needs that can only be met by God. Boasting in God is the only boasting that should be on the lips of a Christ-follower.

Father, I pray You will be quick to convict me when I'm tempted to brag on myself. I long to be someone who sings Your praises all the days of my life. I ask You to free me from the need of self-promotion and to help me rest in Your love.

Have you ever been disappointed when you didn't receive human praise? How does seeking constant approval from others set us up for disaster?

The Value of a Clear Conscience

The wicked flee though no one pursues,
    but the righteous are as bold as a lion.
—*Proverbs 28:1*

A nyone who says, "Time heals all wounds" hasn't lived for decades with a guilty conscience. Those who live with unconfessed sin and guilt are plagued with irrational anxiety. Solomon said, "The wicked flee though no one pursues, but the righteous are as bold as a lion" (v. 1). When people engage in wicked behavior, guilt and fear of being caught follow them wherever they go. They are always mindful that they've broken the law. Like criminals, they run even when no one is chasing them.[66] Undoubtedly, this is a miserable way to live.

On the other hand, Solomon pointed out that righteous people can live with the boldness of a lion. Of course, righteous people sin too. The Bible teaches that all people have fallen short of the glory of God (Romans 3:23). But when the righteous sin, they are quick to confess their sin and be forgiven by God. The apostle John wrote, "If we confess our sins, he is faithful and just and will forgive us our sins and purify us from all unrighteousness" (1 John 1:9). The righteous won't ignore sin in their lives, but rather, will confess it and receive God's forgiveness and restoration. As a result, they can live in complete confidence before God and others. Righteous people don't need to flee from lions or anything else because they know they are right with God in Jesus Christ. Therefore, they can confront any situation with boldness.

People who walk in wisdom and live righteous lives enjoy the abundant life Jesus promised they could have (John 10:10). God's way of living is the most vibrant way. All other paths lead to destruction. Those who walk in wisdom can face each day with courage and anticipation. They can look to the future with hope and joy. When we are committed to seeking God and walking in wisdom, we will avoid falling into the traps set by the wicked (Proverbs 3:25–26) and we will stay far from paths that lead to violence and destruction. When God warns His people to avoid something, He doesn't do so to keep us from enjoyment. Instead, if God prohibits something, He intends to protect us from harm.

Father, I thank You that because of Christ's finished work on the cross, I can confess my sins and be forgiven. I pray I will be quick to repent in areas where I fall into sin so I can live with a clear conscience before You all the days of my life. I pray I will live with boldness and the confidence that comes from knowing I belong to Jesus Christ.

Do you have any unconfessed sin in your past that has caused guilt to linger? What steps can you take to come clean with God? How have you experienced the joys of righteous living? Does your faith result in living with boldness?

The Perils of Flattery

Those who flatter their neighbors
are spreading nets for their feet.
—*Proverbs 29:5*

Read Proverbs 29

A ll of us appreciate a kind word or sincere compliment. A well-timed piece of encouragement can do wonders. But not all compliments come from a place of sincerity. Words of flattery are born from ulterior motives. When we are on the receiving end of flattery, we might enjoy what's being said, but deep down we know something is amiss. Flattery doesn't originate in kindness, but instead, its motive is manipulation.

As king of Israel, David was no stranger to flattery, and he described the flatterer this way: "His talk is smooth as butter, yet war is in his heart; his words are more soothing than oil, yet they are drawn swords" (Psalm 55:21). Flattery's goal is the destruction of others. King Solomon wrote, "Those who flatter their neighbors are spreading nets for their feet" (Proverbs 29:5). Not only were David and Solomon father and son, but they both ruled as king in their perspective eras. People in positions of power are often confronted with flattery because people often approach those in authority with agendas of their own.

Solomon suggested that a person who flatters his neighbor is luring him into a trap with his words.[67] Flattery is a tactic designed to entice the recipient by appealing to his vanity and lowering his guard. The goal of flattery is to manipulate its victim. To complicate matters, there's often a thread of truth in flattering words, which makes it even more appealing to the victim. But flattery exaggerates praise beyond the boundaries of reality. If a person falls for flattery, he will make foolish decisions. "A lying tongue hates those it hurts, and a flattering mouth works ruin" (Proverbs 26:28).

To avoid falling for flattery, we need to ask God to increase our wisdom and to give us sound judgment. Asking for more wisdom is something God's people should do on a continual basis, and the Scriptures encourage us to do so. "If any of you lacks wisdom, you should ask God, who gives generously to all without finding fault, and it will be given to you" (James 1:5). Not only do we need to ask God to give us the wisdom to discern flattery from sincere compliments, but we also need to ask God to remove from us any tendency to use flattery ourselves. Using flattery to manipulate other people is a character flaw that has no place in the life of the believer.

Father, I pray You will increase my wisdom and give me the ability to discern flattery from other types of communication. I pray that You will remove any tendency I might have to use flattery to manipulate other people. I acknowledge it as a sin and want no part of it in my life. I pray I will be neither its perpetrator or victim.

Are you ever tempted to use flattery to get something you want? How do you respond when someone flatters you? Why is flattery so sinister?

God's Word Is Supreme

Every word of God is flawless;
   he is a shield to those who take refuge in him.
Do not add to his words,
   or he will rebuke you and prove you a liar.
—*Proverbs 30:5-6*

Read Proverbs 30

A s we seek to grow in wisdom, we must be mindful that Christ is the source of all wisdom and knowledge (Colossians 2:3). Only in a relationship with Jesus can we grow in wisdom, because no wisdom exists apart from Him. The primary way we grow in our relationship with God is through prayer and the study of His Word. The author of Proverbs 30 described God's Word in its original form as "flawless" (v. 5). If no person can find truth by his own reasoning or intellect, then God is the only infallible source of truth.[68] Those of us who trust God and rely on the truths of His Word will find Him to be a shield for the harsh realities of life in a fallen world.

Studying the Scriptures is the primary way we grow in our understanding of God's character, His redemptive plan for humanity, and where we fit into the grand narrative of God's will. God's Word teaches us the promises God has made to us in Christ, shows us how to live as Christ-followers, and points us to God's plan for eternity. Simply put, it's impossible to have an intimate relationship with Christ apart from the study of His Word. The Bible is our handbook for living, and there is no higher authority than the Word of God.

The apostle Paul made it clear that God's Word was penned by men but was inspired by God and therefore ultimately authored by God. Paul wrote, "All Scripture is God-breathed and is useful for teaching, rebuking, correcting and training in righteousness, so that the servant of God may be thoroughly equipped for every good work" (2 Timothy 3:16–17).

The Word of God is unlike any other book, and the Scriptures have the power to change lives. God's Word gets into the DNA of the believer. The writer of Hebrews described God's Word this way: "For the word of God is alive and active. Sharper than any double-edged sword, it penetrates even to dividing soul and spirit, joints and marrow; it judges the thoughts and attitudes of the heart" (Hebrews 4:12).

Father, I thank You for the incomparable gift of knowing You through Your Word. I pray You will continue to reveal new things to me in the Scriptures. I ask that You teach me things I could not know apart from You. I pray You will give me a supreme love for You and Your Word.

> **Do you commit to spending time each day reading God's Word? What difference have God's promises made in your life? Why is your life different because you engage the Scriptures? In this season of life, which of God's promises are most meaningful to you?**

Speak Up for Those Who Can't

Speak up for those who cannot speak for
themselves,
for the rights of all who are destitute.
Speak up and judge fairly;
defend the rights of the poor and needy.
—*Proverbs 31:8–9*

Read Proverbs 31:1-9

I
t's believed King Lemuel wrote Proverbs 30 and 31. Lemuel means "belonging to God."[69] In the final chapter of Proverbs, King Lemuel shared wisdom communicated to him by his mother, which is a shift from the typical pattern in Proverbs, which primarily deals with the instruction given by a father to his son.

King Lemuel's words speak to the issue of justice. God's people are commanded to speak up for those who can't speak for themselves. In every society, there are people who are poor, oppressed, sick, and marginalized due to their lack of resources. Women and children are always among the most vulnerable. People who fall into these categories lose their voice in the public square because they lack influence and therefore are often overlooked. If legal issues arise, the poor are not able to hire high-powered attorneys to represent them, and consequently, they don't always get a fair hearing in court. Their lack of resources puts them in compromised positions with those who are influential.

King Lemuel understood that his position gave him an opportunity to speak up for those who were not able to plead their case, even though the poor were in no place to reward him. As the king, it was Lemuel's responsibility to judge fairly and give fair treatment to all people, even those who were destitute. As a government official, he could enact decrees to protect the vulnerable and see to it that those laws were enforced. While it's vital that government officials are mindful of the plight of the poor, the care of the poor should never be limited to politicians. Christ's church is called to care for the poor and the marginalized.

Christians should care deeply about issues of justice and lend their voices on behalf of those who can't speak for themselves. Apart from Christ, we are all oppressed due to our sins. How we treat marginalized people tells a lot about how well we understand what God has done for us in the finished work of Jesus Christ. Seeking justice for the marginalized should be a part of every Christ-follower's lifestyle. Micah 6:8 says, "He has shown you, O mortal, what is good. And what does the LORD require of you? To act justly and to love mercy and to walk humbly with your God."

Father, I pray my heart will be tender to the poor and oppressed. I ask You to lead me to specific ways I can serve them. I pray I will be generous with my resources. I pray You will give me opportunities to speak up for those who can't speak for themselves.

What are practical ways you can serve the poor? How can you use your voice to advocate for the oppressed? Which underserved people groups are you drawn to? What difference could you make for them by lending your skill sets and resources to meet their needs?

Noble Character

Charm is deceptive, and beauty is fleeting;
> but a woman who fears the Lord is to be praised.

—*Proverbs 31:30*

Read Proverbs 31:10–31

E arly in the book of Proverbs, Solomon revealed that the "fear of the LORD is the beginning of knowledge" (1:7). As the book comes to a close, King Lemuel, the probable author of Proverbs 30–31, paints a portrait of a woman who "fears the LORD" (31:30). In modern culture, there is an unfortunate emphasis placed on a woman's appearance and very little discussion about the importance of godly character. But King Lemuel wrote, "Beauty is fleeting; but a woman who fears the LORD is to be praised" (v. 30).

The writer described the woman of noble character as one who can make full use of the resources available to her. Because of her integrity, she is a woman of rarity and great value, worth more than rubies (v. 10). One of the most notable assets of her character is her work ethic. In every sense, she is the opposite of the sluggard. She arises early (v. 15), works with eager hands (v. 13), and provides for her family (v. 15). She has wisdom that translates to keen business sense and is described as a woman of strength and dignity (vv. 16, 25). As a result of her excellent work ethic and godly character, "she can laugh at the days to come" (v. 25). Although the coming days may bring uncertainty, she can face them with confidence.[70]

Society places a high premium on a woman's appearance, but the Scriptures make it clear that no woman's beauty will last forever

(v. 30). She has more important priorities than mere outward appearance. Proverbs began with a call for all people to fear the Lord, and it is fitting that it ends with a portrait of a woman who does. When men and women revere God above all other things, other priorities find their place in successive order. When asked about the most important command, Jesus said, "'Love the Lord your God with all your heart and with all your soul and with all your mind and with all your strength.' The second is this: 'Love your neighbor as yourself.' There is no commandment greater than these" (Mark 12:30–31). Placing God at the center of our lives puts everything else in proper perspective.

A reverence for God will motivate our pursuit of wisdom. As we grow in our relationship with Christ, we will experience an increased desire to live the way He intends us to, and we'll come to see with greater clarity that God's way of living is the most vibrant life.

Father, I pray You will teach me to revere You above all things. I ask that You will increase my love for You with each passing day. Help me to grow in wisdom and knowledge of You all the days of my life.

Has your reverence for God grown as you've studied Scripture? Do you love God more today than you did this time last year? Practically speaking, how has God increased your wisdom?

Notes

1. Warren B. Wiersbe, *Be Skillful: God's Guidebook to Wise Living* (Colorado Springs, CO: Cook, 1995), 7–8.
2. Daniel L. Akin and Jonathan Akin, *Christ-Centered Exposition: Exalting Jesus in Proverbs* (Nashville, TN: Holman, 2017), 7.
3. Wiersbe, 23.
4. Max Anders, *Holman Old Testament Commentary: Proverbs* (Nashville, TN: Holman, 1984), 14.
5. HCSB Study Bible (Nashville, TN: Holman, 2010), 1031.
6. Ibid., 1032, 1070.
7. Akin and Akin, 43.
8. Anders, 31.
9. Ibid., 29.
10. Wiersbe, 36–37.
11. Akin and Akin, 53–54.
12. ESV Study Bible (Wheaton, IL: Crossway, 2008), 1142.
13. Wiersbe, 53.
14. Akin and Akin, 75.
15. Anders, 48.
16. Wiersbe, 110.
17. Anders, 51–52.
18. Ibid., 72–73.
19. Akin and Akin, 86.
20. Ibid., 86.
21. Ibid., 88.
22. Ibid., 92–93.
23. Ibid., 96.
24. Ibid., 104–5.
25. Ibid., 105–6.
26. Anders, 106–7.
27. Wiersbe, 185–86.
28. Ibid., 185–86.
29. Anders, 184.
30. Ibid., 115, 118.
31. Ibid., 115, 118.
32. Ibid., 118.
33. Ibid., 197.
34. Ibid., 209, 211.
35. Ibid., 210.
36. Trent C. Butler, *Holman Bible Dictionary* (Nashville, TN, Holman, 1991), 665.
37. Wiersbe, 117–18.
38. Bruce K. Waltke, *The New International Commentary on the Old Testament: The Book of Proverbs Chapters 1–15* (Grand Rapids, MI: Eerdmans, 2004), 607.
39. Ibid., 607.
40. Wiersbe, 136.
41. Ibid., 137.
42. Akin and Akin, 125–26.
43. Ibid., 125–26.
44. Anders, 210.
45. HCSB Study Bible, 1056.
46. Blaise Pascal, *Pensées*, trans. W. F. Trotter (Mineola, NY: Dover, 2013).
47. Akin and Akin, 114–15.
48. Anders, 223.
49. Ibid., 233.
50. Ibid., 233.
51. Ibid., 323–24.
52. Ibid., 324.
53. ESV Study Bible, 518.
54. Anders, 264.
55. Ibid., 264.
56. Ibid., 198.
57. Aimee Groth, "You're the Average of the Five People You Spend the Most Time With," *Business Insider*, July 24, 2012, http://www.businessinsider.com/jim-rohn-youre-the-average-of-the-five-people-you-spend-the-most-time-with-2012-7.
58. ESV Study Bible, 1174.
59. Anders, 327.
60. Bruce K. Waltke, *The New International Commentary on the Old Testament: The Book of Proverbs Chapters 16–31* (Grand Rapids, MI: Eerdmans, 2004), 284.
61. Anders, 290–91.
62. Wiersbe, 103.
63. Anders, 339.
64. Ibid., 337.
65. Ibid., 186.
66. Ibid., 337.
67. Ibid., 221.
68. Ibid., 348.
69. Ibid., 360–61.
70. Ibid., 362–63.